LIGHTING FOR PHOTOGRAPHY

LIGHTING FOR PHOTOGRAPHY

MEANS AND METHODS

WALTER NURNBERG
F.R.P.S., F.I.I.P.

Eighteenth Impression

THE FOCAL PRESS
LONDON AND NEW YORK

ISBN 0 240 50669 3

First printed November 1940

Second Edition March 1942

Third Impression March 1943

Fourth Impression July 1944

Fifth Impression November 1944

Sixth Impression June 1945

Seventh Impression February 1946

Eighth Impression January 1947

Ninth Impression June 1947

Tenth (U.S.) Edition July 1948

Eleventh Revised Edition February 1951

Twelfth Edition October 1953

Thirteenth Edition February 1957

Fourteenth Impression April 1961

Fifteenth Impression July 1965

Sixteenth (Revised) Edition July 1968

Seventeenth Impression February 1971

Eighteenth Impression July 1975

Translated Editions

LA LUMIÈRE ARTIFICIELLE ET LA PHOTOGRAPHIE
Éditions Prisma, Paris

LA ILUMINACIÓN EN LA FOTOGRAFÍA
Ediciones Omega, Barcelona

LICHT UND BELEUCHTUNG IN DER FOTOGRAFIE
Wilhelm Knapp Verlag, Düsseldorf

BELYSNINGSTEKNIK
Skrifola Limited, Copenhagen

Printed in Great Britain by Billing & Sons Limited, Guildford and London and bound by W. & J. Mackay & Co. Limited, Chatham.

CONTENTS

FOREWORD TO THE SIXTEENTH EDITION 9

I. *THE THEORY OF LIGHT* 11

LIGHT AND THE PHOTOGRAPHIC EMULSION 12
    Light—What it is 12
    The Visible Spectrum 12
    The Colour of Light 13
    The Effect of Colour on the Monochrome Negative 14
    The Reproduction of Colours in Terms of Monochrome . . . 16
    Light Filters 17

LIGHT AND COLOUR PHOTOGRAPHY 20
    Colour Balance 20
    Exposure Duration and Speed 22
    Colour Filters in Colour Photography 23
        Colour-correcting Filters 23
        Light-balancing Filters 23
        Colour-compensating Filters 24
        Colour-printing Filters 24
    Colour Filters for Colour Photography 25

LIGHT AND THE SUBJECT 26
    Photometric Units 26
    Reflection 27
    Absorption of Light 28
    The Refraction of Light 29
    The Colour of Our Subjects 31

II. *THE MEANS OF LIGHTING* 33

ELECTRICITY 34
    Electric Units 34
    Capacity of Installation 35
    Fuses 36
    Direct and Alternating Current 36
    Resistances and Dimmers 37
    Chokes and Transformers 37

PHOTOGRAPHIC LIGHT SOURCES 39
    Quality and Quantity of Light 40
    Types of Light Sources 40
    Tungsten Filament Lamps 40
    Integral Reflector Lamps 42
    Tungsten–Halogen Lamps 43
    Carbon-arc Lighting 43
    Electronic Flash 44
    Flash-bulbs 45
    Electronic Flash and Expendable Flash Compared 48

LIGHTING UNITS 49
    Reflectors 49
    Flood-lights 52
    Spot-lights 52
    Flood- and Spot-lights Compared 55
    The Colortran Lighting System 56
    Indirect Lighting 57
    Lighting Outfit for Studio and Home 58
    Equipping a Studio 61
    Lamp-stands and Fixtures 61

THE ESTIMATION OF EXPOSURE 65
    Exposing Monochrome Materials 65
    Brightness Range and Development 65
    Factors Determining Exposure 66
    Exposing Colour Materials 68
    Determination of Exposure 68
    Exposure Meters 68
    Filter Factors 69
    Exposure Estimation with Flash 70
    Electronic Flash in the Studio 72

III. THE PRINCIPLES OF LIGHTING 73
BUILDING UP THE LIGHTING 74
    The Direction of Light 75
    Terms 76
    The First Step: Visualising 76
    The Second Step: The Basic Light 81
    The Third Step: The Supplementary Light 81
    Background Projection 82
    Daylight 82
    Primitive Light Sources 83

THE SHADOW 93
    Types of Shadows 93
    The Tone of the Cast Shadow 94
    Definition of the Cast Shadow 96
    Shape and Size of a Cast Shadow 97
    Dominance of Cast Shadows 98
    The Bogus Shadow 99

The Annexed Cast Shadow 100
The Isolated Shadow. 105
The Silhouette Shadow 105
Other Kinds of Isolated Cast Shadow 107
Shadow-free Treatments 107
High Key Photography 107
Shadow-free Background Photography 109

IV. *THE APPLICATION OF LIGHTING* 113
LIGHT AND SHADOW AS APPLIED TO FACE AND FIGURE . . 114
The Profile 116
    Pure Silhouette 116
    Semi-silhouette 121
    Dark-outline Lighting 121
    Rim Effect 121
    Cross-light 122
    Central Light 123
The Three-quarter Face 123
    Semi-silhouette 124
    Cross-light 124
    Side-light 141
    Central light 142
The Full Face 143
    Central Light 143
    Double-rim Light 144
    Cross-light 145
Lighting a Figure 145
    The Nude 146
    The Dressed Figure 146
Hints on the Lighting of Groups 148
The Lighting of Hands 158

LIGHT AND SHADOW AS APPLIED TO THE INANIMATE . . . 161
The Reproduction of Flat Originals 161
Rendering Textures 162
    Fabrics 163
    Leather 164
    Paper 174
    Flowers 175
Reflecting Surfaces 176
Reflection and Catchlights. 176
    Wood 181
    Pottery 182
    Glassware 182
    Silver and other Metals 184
Lighting in Illustrative Industrial Photography 201
    Photographing Machinery 202
    The Figure in Industry. 203
    Hands in Industry 204
    The Long View 204
    Industry in Colour 205
    General Considerations 205

INDEX 207

FOREWORD TO THE SIXTEENTH EDITION

The last few years have brought many changes to photography. The manufacturers of photographic equipment and materials have given us many new tools and have perfected old ones. In the field of lighting, the wide use of electronic flash, quartz iodine lamps and integral reflector bulbs have proved their success.

And, of course, there is colour! Although technical and aesthetic development is going on all the time, colour photography has long been a medium in its own right and a valuable commercial commodity.

This edition, therefore, includes much new material and it is here that I wish to express my grateful thanks to my colleague Mr. Michael Langford, F.I.I.P., F.R.P.S., who has contributed valuable information.

I believe that this new edition is timely. Apart from commercial considerations, the inherent attractiveness of colour has, in recent years, tempted many to prefer it to black and white. The latter has always required that imaginative effort in terms of lighting to lift it out of the ordinary and the fact that this special effort is now often lacking, begins to make itself felt.

Similarly there is little doubt that the convenient means of electronic flash and its power to freeze action, has led many to rely less on creative thought than on the ability of their models to produce a continuous change of action and expression, in the sure knowledge that at least a few of the many exposures will prove to be visually exciting and meaningful—however accidentally produced.

This new—to me somewhat haphazard—approach has made a valid contribution to illustrative photography. But this does not mean that it should be allowed to put an end to creative intent and ability. New inventions and techniques must do more than merely add a few new gimmicks to old ones.

Progress surely means that experience accumulated over a long period can be seen in perspective and be combined to deepen the power of expression and broaden the scope of photography in all illustrative fields.

London, 1968   *WALTER NURNBERG*

KEY TO LIGHTING DIAGRAMS

Sitter	●	♀	Flood, pointing up
Camera	⌂	◉	Flood, pointing down
Camera, pointing down	⌂	∿	Flood with diffuser
Camera, pointing up	⌂	∿∿	Bank of Floods
Window, small	⊥	◁	Spot-light
Window, normal	⊥⊥	◖◗	Spot-light, pointing up
Window, large	⊥⊥⊥	◖◗	Spot-light, pointing down
Reflector	▭	○	Ordinary electric bulb
Mirror	▭	☼	Sun
Flood	▽	☀	Sun, low

10

I THE THEORY OF LIGHT

A more apt definition of the word photography than the etymo-logical "writing with light" would be *painting with light.* If light is our paint, and the sensitive emulsion our canvas, then it is necessary, before one can become a master of the craft, to investigate the nature of these materials; for while the outdoor photographer finds his paint ready mixed for him by the sun, the indoor worker, like the old masters, has to mix it himself.

Upon his knowledge of its ingredients will depend the success of his work.

LIGHT—WHAT IT IS

Visible light forms a very small proportion—less than one octave—of an enormous gamut, totalling about twenty octaves, of so-called *electro-magnetic waves*, which permeate space, and which travel at the incredible velocity of 186,300 miles per second. The distance from the crest of one wave to the crest of the next is called the *wave-length*, a term which radio has made familiar to us all, and which is mathematically linked with the *frequency*.

The wave-lengths of this enormous range of waves are measured in terms of the *micron* (μ) which equals $\frac{1}{1000}$ mm.; the *millimicron* ($\mu\mu$), or millionth of a millimetre; or the Ångström unit (Å or ÅU), which is equal to one ten-millionth of a millimetre; and in the other direction, in ascending units to thousands of metres. Only vibrations of a wave-length between 4000 and 7000 Å (400 to 700 $\mu\mu$ or 0·4 to 0·7 μ) are perceptible to the eye, and these, together with the neighbouring infra-red and ultra-violet rays, are termed *light*.

THE VISIBLE SPECTRUM

It is necessary to consider rather more closely that band of wave-lengths known as the visible spectrum.

If we pass a beam of sunlight through a prism and then intercept the light thus transmitted, we shall observe, not a white patch of light, but a light-beam which has been broken up into a continuous band of different colours like a rainbow. This band, which we call the *spectrum*, includes an infinite number of hues, ranging from crimson red—which is least bent by the prism—to violet, which is refracted at the most oblique angle. The principal hues in between the crimson-red and the violet are: vermilion-red, orange, yellow, green and blue.

Besides these visible vibrations, two other kinds of *invisible* rays are contained in that compound which makes up "white light": ultra-violet and infra-red rays. Although these two radiations are not visible to the naked eye, and are therefore called the invisible spectrum, they can under certain conditions be registered by photographic emulsions. (See p. 16.)

THE COLOUR OF LIGHT

We now see that "white light" is in reality nothing but a conglomeration of the different colours contained in the spectrum *plus* ultra-violet (wavelengths under 4000 ÅU) and infra-red (wave-lengths over 7000 ÅU).

To simplify the matter *we may divide the visible spectrum into three bands: the blue band; the green band; the red band.*

The principal components of the three colour-bands are as follows:

In the blue band
    violet with a wave-length of 4000 to 4500 ÅU.
    blue   „   „   4500 „ 5000 ÅU.
In the green band
    green with a wave-length of 5000 to 5600 ÅU.
    yellow   „   „   5600 „ 5900 ÅU.
In the red band
    orange with a wave-length of 5900 to 6400 ÅU.
    red   „   „   6400 „ 7200 ÅU.

It must be clearly understood that the above-mentioned colours do not stand well defined "side by side" in the spectrum, but that they are connected and blended into each other by further intermediate colours, hues which are mixtures of each of the neighbouring colours. For instance, there are several shades of blue-violet between blue and violet, several shades of blue-green between blue and green, and so forth.

Blue, green and red are called primary colours because with them any other colour may be synthesised. If one mixes *the three primary colours in equal quantities, white light will be produced.* Midday sunlight is thus white light because it contains the three colour **wave-bands** in equal proportions.

It is only logical that if these proportions are altered the colour of the light too will be altered. For instance, light produced by our electric bulbs, although still being a kind of "white light", is actually much more red than the light produced by noon sunlight. The reason for this is that approximately 50% of this light is transmitted on the red wave-band, 30% on the green wave-band and only 20% on the blue wave-band—provided the bulb is being burnt at its normal voltage. (See p. 40.)

If such an alteration of the proportions of the different colour-bands in the spectrum makes a clearly visible difference in the colour impression, it is obvious that one can produce any desired colour if one succeeds in getting rid more or less of certain colours contained in the spectrum. In short, a given colour is the result of having omitted some other colours (or colour) from the complete spectrum.

Any colour can be abstracted from white light by the use of a transparent medium of suitable colour. Thus, to remove the surplus red from the light of our ordinary electric bulb, we have to use a screen which will abstract red; reference to the table of colour-bands (on p. 13) will suggest that such a screen must transmit violet, blue, green and yellow. In effect, such a screen (or filter) would be blue-green in colour, and since this colour abstracts red, *blue-green* is known as *minus-red*, and red and blue-green, which together make up white light, are known as *complementary colours.*

Similarly, a mixture of blue-violet and red-orange, or magenta, will intercept the green rays, and consequently *magenta* is known as *minus-green.* A mixture of green, yellow, orange and red will abstract blue, and consequently *yellow* is known as *minus-blue.* Green and magenta are complementary colours, and so are blue and yellow.

THE EFFECT OF COLOUR
ON THE MONOCHROME NEGATIVE

In ordinary monochrome photography, colours are replaced by different degrees of brightness between white and black. As a matter of fact, the brightness of the colours can be estimated by their reflection coefficients.

Orange reflects, for example, approximately 62%, green approximately 25%, blue-green approximately 15%, vermilion approximately 15%, cobalt blue approximately 15%, ultra-marine blue approximately 12%.

These figures, however, have not much practical importance for the photographer, as there is not yet a photographic negative material available which "sees" colours as does the human eye.

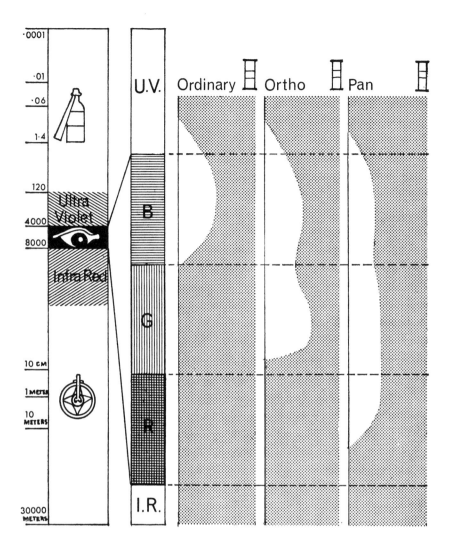

The spectrum and the effect of colour. The *column on the left* indicates the ether spectrum: in its top third the position of the radiation (X-rays, gamma-rays), so useful for medical purposes, is indicated; in its lower half the approximate position of heat and radio waves is pointed out; the area of the visible spectrum is about in the centre, with the ultra-violet and the infra-red bands over and under it. In the *next column* we find the visible spectrum proportionately enlarged and split up into the blue, green and red components. The following *three columns* show how far films of the three principal types react to the colours of the visible and invisible photographic spectrum, the white curves showing *the* intensity of response by the films in question.

15

Moreover, almost every type of negative material registers colours in its own particular way. The *colour sensitivity* of our plates and films is everything but uniform.

The colour sensitivity of an emulsion is expressed in terms of wave-lengths, and is in practice illustrated by means of *wedge spectrograms*, which, although they may look highly abstruse, actually illustrate graphically the sensitivity of the emulsion to the various wave-lengths of light. A number of these spectrograms relating to different types of emulsions are reproduced; it will be seen that the figures along the scale represent the wave-length (in hundreds of Ångstroms), and the height of the spectrogram at any point represents the sensitivity of the emulsion to light of that wave-length.

While many practical photographers are apt to regard such data as mere scientific curiosities, it is well worth while mastering their meaning. Even in relatively unscientific matters, such as portraiture, they will enable one to answer questions as to how the colour of the sitter's dress will reproduce; they are of immense value in making an intelligent use of filters (see p. 17) and of different light sources (see p. 40).

The *ordinary* old-type negative material registers blue—for the human eye the darkest colour—as the lightest; this will be apparent from p. 15.

This exaggeration of the blue is in fact so great that an ordinary plate or film is completely blind to the difference between the blue of the sky and the white of the clouds. Other colours are not registered at all, not even those which the eye perceives as the brightest, *i.e.* green, yellow and orange.

The negative materials which are sensitive from violet up to yellow-green and also for a part of the ultra-violet are generally known as *orthochromatic;* those sensitive to all colours of the visible spectrum plus ultra-violet as *panchromatic.* The extension of sensitivity is clear from their spectrograms.

Modern science has also produced negative materials sensitive to the vibrations of the *invisible* spectrum; one kind responds exclusively to ultra-violet rays down to wave-length of 1200 Å, another to infra-red rays up to 10,000 Å (heat waves). The usefulness of these two latter negative materials has so far been strictly limited to certain specialised fields of scientific and outdoor photography.

THE REPRODUCTION OF COLOURS
IN TERMS OF MONOCHROME

We have already seen that the *ordinary* material is practically colour-blind. The only colours it does see, violet and blue, are misrepresented to such an extent that this ordinary negative material is useful only for the reproduction of black-and-white objects.

Orthochromatic emulsions, although predominantly susceptible to violet and blue, register also green, yellow-green and yellow but are blind to orange and red. To overcome this divergence between our own vision and that of the camera we must use a filter (see pp. 17 & 18) which absorbs the superfluous influx of ultra-violet, violet and blue light without losing anything of the yellow-green. Except for infrequent, specific purposes orthochromatic materials are now only rarely used, because the modern panchromatic emulsions serve most purposes much better.

Panchromatic materials register all colours and particularly render red approximately correctly, whilst they have not the human eye's exaggerated sensitivity to green. The use of a yellow filter is therefore still essential for outdoor work and for rare special occasions in the studio.

As we shall see later, panchromatic emulsions, in combination with various filters, make it not only possible to represent a colour-impression at its true monochromatic value, but also to "fake" the colours of the object according to our will. This "faking", or exaggeration of colour differences, is, for instance, most helpful when reproducing coloured patterns in which the colours have the same tone-values, and where it is therefore necessary to create an artificial contrast in order to avoid a grey, colourless effect and to inform the spectator that there were different colours on the original.

LIGHT FILTERS

As far as black-and-white work in artificial light is concerned, the principal applications of filters are to improve the rendering of colours, and to obtain a more natural scale of brightnesses, in which case the filter is known as a *correcting filter;* or to increase the difference in rendering of various colours, in which case the filter is known as a *contrast filter.*

A light filter can be put either directly in front of the lens, or directly in front of the light source. In either case the colour medium is usually dyed gelatine; for use on the light source it is generally mounted in a frame, or just slipped into slots provided on the lamp housing.

In filters intended to be used on the lens, the gelatine is usually cemented between two pieces of optical glass, and mounted in a ring clipping to the lens mount. Lens filters must receive the same careful treatment as the lens itself.

As we have already learnt (see p. 14), the term "complementary colour" describes that colour which produces white light when mixed with the colour (or colours) to which it is complementary. For

B

CHARACTERISTICS OF LIGHT FILTERS

Colour	Filter No. Agfa	Gevaert	Ilford	Wratten	Approx. Factor Pan	Red Pan	Colours Absorbed (Darker)	Colours Rendered Lighter
Visually opaque	—	R 719	206	88A	For use with infra-red materials only			Red
Deep red	—	R 619	205	29 (F)	10–20	8–12	All except red	Red
Red	—	R 599	204	25 (A)	7–10	3–5	Violet, blue, green	Orange, red
Red-orange	42	R 586	203	23A (E)	4	3	Violet, blue, green	Orange, red
Orange	6	R 578	202	22	3	2	Violet, blue	Orange, red
Deep yellow	5	6	109	15 (G)	2	$1\frac{1}{2}$	Violet, blue	Yellow to red
Mid-yellow	4	3.4	105, 108	9 (K3)	2	$1\frac{1}{2}$	Violet, some blue	Yellow to red
Light yellow	2	1.2	102, 104	8 (K2)	$1\frac{1}{2}$	$1\frac{1}{2}$	Violet	Yellow to red
Yellow-green	—	—	401	—	$1\frac{1}{2}$	$1\frac{1}{2}$	Violet, some blue, red	Green, yellow
Light green	—	—	402	11 (XI)	3–4	4–5	Violet, some blue, red	Green, yellow
Green	71	G 525	404	58 (B2)	4–6	7–12	Violet, blue, orange, red	Green
Blue contrast	—	B 488	304	47 (B)	10–20	15–25	Yellow, orange, red	Violet, blue
Light blue	—	—	301	38	—	$1\frac{1}{2}$	Red	(Tungsten light correction)
Magenta contrast	—	MG 549	501	33, 34	12	12	Green, yellow	Blue, red

This table shows the characteristics of the more generally used filters of the main manufacturers. The filters grouped in each section, while not strictly speaking identical, have for most practical purposes similar characteristics within the visible spectrum. The filter factors (see p. 69) shown are for correct panchromatic (ortho-panchromatic) and red-panchromatic emulsions, for exposure to tungsten-filament lighting (see p. 40). Where no filter factor is shown, a test should be made with the particular emulsion and illuminant to be employed, since the omission indicates that the factor may vary widely.

18

instance: red complements blue-green, yellow-green complements violet, yellow complements indigo.

From this it follows that the beam of "white light", after having been transmitted through a flat piece of coloured glass or coloured gelatine, takes on the colour of the transmitting medium intercepting it. The reason for this is that *only those light-rays have been transmitted through the light-filter which are not complementary to its own colour, while the complementary colours have been partially or totally absorbed by it.*

A *deep orange filter*, for example, transmits freely only that part of the colour waveband which lies between 5900 Å and infra-red, *i.e.,* deep yellow, orange, vermilion, crimson- red and infra-red. Rays of a wave-length between 5800 and 5500 Å (*i.e.* yellow to yellow-green) are progressively absorbed towards the lower wave-length, while the remaining part of the spectrum, from green to ultra-violet is, for all practical purposes, fully absorbed. Light filtered through an orange filter will render a blue and a green object darker, while red is rendered slightly and yellow considerably lighter. (This and similar information is based on the assumption that a panchromatic material is being used.)

It is not within the scope of this book to discuss the complexities of colour vision or to cover in detail the theory of colour photography. The reader should study these subjects by referring to the special literature devoted to them.

For our purposes it is sufficient to know that all modern colour photography materials are basically of "tripack" construction, *i.e.* that they consist of three emulsion layers which are coated one on top of the other and respond to blue light, green light and red light respectively, and which are critically arranged so that together they give a balanced colour image.

COLOUR BALANCE

The tripack nature of colour materials means that the sensitivity of each emulsion must be critically adjusted in speed and contrast relative to the other layers. If this balance is disturbed one layer may produce too much or too little dye, and the overall result will show a "colour cast". Such casts are particularly noticeable in highlights, neutral greys and pale colours.

The film manufacturers can only balance emulsion characteristics if they assume that their product is to be exposed under a predetermined type of lighting. Herein lies a major difference between the eye, which quickly adapts to a variety of "white" light sources, and tripacks which cannot similarly adapt their sensitivity to the prevailing subject illumination.

In referring to the distribution of wave-lengths emitted by a "white" light source it is easiest to quote the temperature ("Absolute" scale) of a black metal body heated until the colour of the light it emits matches the source in question. This gives us one simple figure which is expressed in degrees Kelvin and is known as the colour temperature of the light source. For example, if the prescribed metal has to be heated to a temperature of 2927° C (= 3200° A) to match the mixture of wave-lengths emitted from a particular tungsten filament the colour temperature of this source is 3200° K. Rather like heating a poker to red and then blue heat, the proportion of blue content increases with colour temperature. Daylight (an average mixture of sky and sunlight) is quoted at 6500° K, whilst a domestic 60 watt lamp may have a colour temperature of 2800° K.

Daylight and Type D films (or Type T, German products) are materials balanced for subject lighting of 6500° K. That is average daylight, or blue flash-bulbs, or most types of electronic flash.

Type A materials (*e.g.* Kodachrome type A) are intended for use with photoflood tungsten light sources of 3400° K.

Type B materials (*e.g.* Ektachrome type B) should be used with photopearl colour-corrected studio lamps of 3200° K.

Some interchange between these emulsions and light sources is possible with the use of conversion filters discussed on page 24.

Even though the correct light source may be chosen for the film in use, colour casts may still result from

(1) Shooting in daylight during early morning or evening conditions, or in shade where light reaches the subject from a blue sky only.

(2) Using aged lamps or lamps in reflectors which are stained or painted other than white.

(3) Light reaching the subject via reflection from coloured surfaces such as walls.

(4) Using electric light sources at other than the specified voltage (voltage reduction of 10% = 4% reduction in colour temperature).

Where a light source is suspected of causing a colour cast it may be visually compared with a source of known colour temperature. More accurately a colour temperature meter can be pointed at a suspected tungsten light source and the colour temperature read directly.

The permissible variation in colour temperature is least with reversal colour materials (approximately ±100° K under studio lighting for critical subjects such as familiar foods, technical subjects, etc.). Colour negative materials have a wider colour temperature latitude (some "universal" types may be exposed to daylight *or* tungsten lighting) as some compensation is possible by filtering in the enlarger. Wherever possible we should try to use lighting at the manufacturer's specified colour temperature.

Fluorescent tubes and other light sources not based on incandescent filaments are usually deficient in certain wave-lengths. Although they may emit some blue and red light (and thus give a

21

colour temperature meter reading) such gaps in their spectrum will almost certainly produce an unsatisfactory result.

Above all a *mixture* of light sources of differing colour temperatures should be avoided in objective colour photography. Obviously no one camera filtration can correct for such a mixed situation. The resulting photograph will show variations in colour balance over differing parts of the subject. Under the photographer's control, however, local colour casts can sometimes be used for subjective effects.

EXPOSURE DURATION AND SPEED

We have seen that the colour temperature of light sources, whilst of only marginal importance in black-and-white work, has a decisive influence on the results of colour photography. Similarly the actual *duration of exposure* must be considered more closely by the colour photographer.

It is well known that irrespective of the normal reciprocal relationship between lens aperture setting and shutter speed, very long exposures to dimly lit subjects or very brief exposures to brilliant subjects both tend to result in underexposure. In other words, an emulsion's quoted speed will hold good only within a range of exposure durations—for example, between 1/250th sec. and 1 sec. Frequently this is accompanied by a change in the emulsion's contrast characteristics. At very long exposures contrast tends to increase and with very short exposures contrast decreases.

This *reciprocity failure* is not of great practical importance in typical black-and-white photography, unless astronomical or high-speed flash work is undertaken. In a colour film, however, extra exposure is needed to counteract both an overall speed loss and a serious alteration of *colour balance*.

The limitations of exposure duration and range are therefore critical in colour photography. Manufacturers publish exposure time recommendations for each colour film—sometimes for individual batches. These either indicate the number of stops extra exposure required, or quote different ASA ratings for typical exposure durations.

A compensation filter may be recommended to help deal with the shift of colour balance.

Wherever possible the photographer should adjust the level of subject illumination until—at the aperture he requires for depth of field—the exposure duration tallies with the manufacturer's recommendations. Some colour films (*i.e.* Ektacolor) are marketed in two forms: type "S" for exposure durations of 1/10th sec. or less, and type "L" adjusted for exposures longer than 1/10th sec.

Colour materials are inherently slower than most black-and-white emulsions. High-speed colour films, whilst still a fraction of the speed of fast black-and-white materials, share their tendency towards visible graininess.

COLOUR FILTERS IN COLOUR PHOTOGRAPHY

Dust-and grease-free lens and filter surfaces, combined with regular use of a lens hood are of special importance in colour work. Light scatter from coloured surfaces outside the subject area otherwise mysteriously degrade contrast and colour balance.

Colour filters for use with colour materials have various overlapping purposes. For clarity we can divide them into (1) colour-correcting filters, (2) light-balancing filters, (3) colour-compensating filters, and (4) colour-printing filters.

Colour-correcting Filters

These filters are marketed by film manufacturers to allow film balanced for one type of illumination to be used under conditions appropriate to another colour balance, *e.g.* to allow type "A" material to be exposed in daylight. In this instance the filter colour would be brownish to correct the dominant blue content of daylight. Conversely filters to allow the use of daylight film in tungsten lighting are blue in colour.

Although colour correcting filters are used in front of the lens, non-photographic acetate filters in rolls 53 in. wide are available for use in front of windows to convert the incident daylight to the colour temperature of the tungsten illumination used inside. These filters, which must *not* be used in front of a lens, mark easily by fingerprints and have to be handled with care. To convert incident daylight (or arc) to 3200° K the Kodak Studio Filter Type E, No. NP 558/13 is standard, whilst to convert 3200° K lighting to be suitable for daylight film stock Filter No. NP 548/2 should be placed in front of the artificial light sources.

The rolls of acetate film are available in lengths of 25 ft. or 50 ft. The material is also available in sheets of 21 in. × 25 in. or 29 in. × 31 in.

The use of correction filters is not as efficient as using appropriately balanced film owing to effective speed losses. Manufacturers publish exposure factors or adjusted emulsion speeds for use with their filters.

Light-balancing Filters

These are useful for controlling the colour of a light source when it is not possible to operate the lamp at the correct colour tempera-

Film Type	Filter Type			
	Photopearl (3200° K)	Photoflood (3400° K)	Clear Flash (3800° K)	Daylight and "Fill In" Blue Flash
Type B (3200° K)	—	Kodak 81 A Gevaert CTO2	Kodak 81 C Gevaert CTO4	Kodak 85B Gevaert CTO12 Agfa K19
Type A (3400° K)	Kodak 82A	—	Kodak 81 C	Kodak 85 Ilford 161
Daylight (6000° K)	Agfa K69 Kodak 80B & 82A* Gevaert CTB12	Kodak 80B*	Kodak 80C* Gevaert CTB8	—

* Kodak recommend that these filters be used in emergency only, as results may not equal the use of appropriately balanced film.
Wherever possible use filters made by the manufacturer of the film.
For effective speed losses see instructions packed with film.

ture. A light-balancing filter can be an acetate sheet used over individual light sources or, if all lights around the set are similarly at fault, in the form of a higher quality gelatine filter over the lens.

Colour-compensating Filters

A wide range of pale filters in yellow, magenta, cyan, red, green and blue are made, primarily to change the overall colour balance of results with colour films. For a combination of reasons the overall colour of a transparency made in the camera or by duplication can prove unsatisfactory. By viewing the result through various colour-compensating filters, it may be possible to achieve visually the required balance. A filter of the same colour and value should then be used over the camera lens in reshooting.

Colour-printing Filters

These are usually made of low quality gelatine for use between the light source and condenser of an enlarger. They include a range of colours similar to compensating filters, and allow control of colour balance when printing colour negatives.

KODAK LIGHT-BALANCING FILTERS

To Bring Colour Temperature to 3200° K
(Required for Type "B" Materials)

C.T. of Source In Use	Wratten Filter No. Required	Approx. Exposure Increase in Stops
2800° K	82C (bluish)	$\frac{2}{3}$
2900° K	82B (,,)	$\frac{2}{3}$
3000° K	82A (,,)	$\frac{1}{2}$
3100° K	82 (,,)	$\frac{1}{3}$
3200° K	—	—
3300° K	81 (brownish)	$\frac{1}{3}$
3400° K	81A (,,)	$\frac{1}{3}$
3500° K	81B (,,)	$\frac{1}{2}$
3600° K	81C (,,)	$\frac{1}{2}$
3850° K	81EF (,,)	$\frac{2}{3}$

To Bring Colour Temperature to 3400° K
(Required for Type "A" Materials)

C.T. of Source In Use	Wratten Filter No. Required	Approx. Exposure Increase in Stops
2950° K	82C (bluish)	$\frac{2}{3}$
3060° K	82B (,,)	$\frac{2}{3}$
3180° K	82A (,,)	$\frac{1}{2}$
3290° K	82 (,,)	$\frac{1}{3}$
3400° K	—	—
3510° K	81 (brownish)	$\frac{1}{3}$
3630° K	81A (,,)	$\frac{1}{3}$
3740° K	81B (,,)	$\frac{1}{2}$
3850° K	81C (,,)	$\frac{1}{2}$
4140° K	81EF (,,)	$\frac{2}{3}$

COLOURLESS FILTERS FOR COLOUR PHOTOGRAPHY

A polarising filter or pola screen, whilst of value in certain applications of black and white photography, offers special advantages in colour work (see page 176).

Ultra-violet absorbing filters can be useful in absorbing shortwave radiation when shooting outdoors in open shade, at high altitudes or over water. The blue sensitive layer of tripack materials in particular responds to ultra-violet and the final photograph may reveal a distinct blue haze unless this colourless filter is used. No increase in exposure is normally needed.

Light becomes visible and usable for photographic purposes only when it is intercepted by some substance and is reflected from it. Dust in the atmosphere is already sufficient to make light perceptible to vision. It follows that an object becomes visible only when it reflects the light which falls on it. This statement does not mean, however, that the object has to reflect the same amount of light as is caught by its surface; it is always a fact that only a certain part of the light is *reflected*, while the rest is *absorbed* or "sucked up".

The lightness or darkness of a given surface depends mainly on two factors.

The first is the *quantity of light which is received* by it, this factor being governed by the brightness and intensity of the light source and by the distance of this light source from the object. *The efficacy of illumination is inversely proportional to the square of the distance.* Thus, placing a lamp of 100 watts at a distance of 3 ft. from a given object (or screen) produces the same intensity of illumination as a lamp of 900 watts placed at a distance of 9 ft.

The second factor is the coefficient of reflection—meaning, in plain language, that *percentage of light which is reflected* from a surface.

PHOTOMETRIC UNITS

We thus have three quantities to consider in the measurement of light for photography: (1) *the total quantity of light emitted by the source;* (2) the *intensity* (not the quantity) *of light falling on the subject;* (3) *the intensity of light reflected back from the subject.*

(1) The accepted unit for all photometric units is the *international candle*—actually the light emitted by a candle made to very exact specifications. The emission of this source is the *candle-power* (c.p.).

(2) If we take a surface having an area of 1 sq. ft., and place it at a distance of 1 ft.

from our candle, it will receive a total light flux of 1 *lumen*. The intensity of light falling on the surface will be 1 *foot-candle*.

Now, if we place our surface at a distance of 2 ft. from the source, it will, by the inverse-square law, receive only $\frac{1}{4}$ lumen of light, and will receive an intensity of only $\frac{1}{4}$ foot-candle. If, however, we take a surface of 4 sq. ft. and place it 2 ft. from the source, then it will receive again a total of 1 lumen; but the intensity will be unaltered at $\frac{1}{4}$ foot-candle.

(3) The reflection of light from an illuminated surface is measured by the *foot-lambert*. If our surface is 1 ft. from the source, and hence receives an illumination of 1 foot-candle, and if, furthermore, we assume it to be a completely diffusing surface, with a reflectivity of, say, 90%, then the brightness of the surface will be 0·9 foot-lambert. As we shall shortly see, however, no surface is completely diffusing, and actually the reflection will vary according to the direction in which the measurement is taken.

REFLECTION

We have to distinguish between two main kinds of reflection: *concentrated or specular reflection* and *diffused reflection.*

Concentrated or *specular reflection* means that the light-beam which falls upon a surface is reflected back without being scattered.

Diffused reflection implies that the light-beam is broken up, or scattered in all directions, at the moment of incidence.

This classification describes only the most extreme effects of reflection, and there is, between these two antipodal types, a wide variety of "in-between" reflections which combine in themselves the properties of both extremes in varying degrees.

The extent to which a reflection is concentrated or diffused depends on the kind and structure of the reflecting surface. *The smoother and more highly polished that surface is, the more concentrated will be the reflection; the duller and more textural the surface, the more diffused will be the reflection.*

The ideal surfaces for producing a specular or concentrated reflection are provided by materials such as plate-glass mirrors, shiny and perfectly flat metal sheets, etc. On the other hand, surfaces such as white plaster walls, grainy matt cardboards or white blotting-paper are the best bases for diffused reflections.

Materials such as glazed boards, matt metal surfaces—*e.g.* matted aluminium sheets, etc.—provide reflections which lie between the concentrated and the completely diffused reflection and which will demonstrate therefore, in a varying degree, a strongly marked direction of reflection while at the same time another part of the light-rays is freely dispersed.

In the case of specular reflection, the *angle of reflection is equal to the angle of incidence.* In order to make the implications of this clear, one just has to imagine a tennis ball being thrown to the ground at some angle or other. It will be observed—provided the ball has been thrown without a spin—that it rebounds at an angle which corresponds exactly with the angle of its incidence.

Actually the same law applies to the case of diffused reflection, but the beam of light is split up into so great a number of individual rays that the reflection is dispersed in all directions. As mentioned, there are instances where the greater part of the total amount of reflection is bounced back at the angle of incidence, while a smaller portion is scattered about haphazardly.

These considerations are of some practical consequence. They not only influence lighting technique, but also the choice of camera angle.

This does *not* apply when we have to deal with a completely diffused reflection, as then the light is split up and redistributed in all directions in equal proportions thus producing an extensive field of even illumination which can be viewed from nearly every angle without altering its appearance.

But when we have to cope with a concentrated reflection we shall see that the direction of the reflected light-beam is strongly marked and the field of illumination strictly limited. If our camera is to register this concentrated reflection, it is essential that the concentrated reflected light-beam is caught by the lens. It follows that, if the "width" of the reflection is only narrow, the lens must face, more or less, the direction from which the reflection is thrown.

The more we widen the angle between the line of reflection and the line of camera-vision, the less reflection will be registered on our negative.

ABSORPTION OF LIGHT

We have already heard that a surface never reflects the same amount of light as it receives, but that a certain amount of it is always absorbed. *The more light reflected the lighter will the surface appear; the less light reflected the darker will it seem.*

Unfortunately, our naked eye can only distinguish relative luminosities in a rather rough manner. Although we can say that one thing is lighter or darker than another when seeing them side by side, we are rather vague in our judgment of tone values; we can perceive the relation of one tone to another, but cannot exactly estimate the extent of it.

Everyone who has ever handled a camera knows how easy it is to be deceived in this respect, and everyone has been surprised to find a negative under- or over-exposed although at the time of exposure the lighting conditions might have seemed entirely reliable. The human eye has the wonderful faculty of being able to adapt itself only too willingly to changing lighting conditions, though it may need some time to adjust itself. Every photographer will have experienced how a comparatively weak light dazzles him when coming out of a dark-room and how consequently the brightness of the light gets easily over-valued.

Luckily, once again science has come to the rescue of our erring judgment. Detailed information on the coefficient of reflection, relating to different kinds of surfaces, is available.

Apart from a mirror, which can produce only a directionally concentrated reflection, the strongest reflection of light is obtained from freshly smoked magnesium oxide. This "whitest" material is the international standard with which the reflectances of all other white materials are compared.

A magnesium oxide surface carefully prepared will reflect 100% of the incident light. Natural chalk reflects 97% and white plaster 95%. More familiar materials such as white paint have reflectances between 85 and 93%, white blotting paper 92% and other white papers between 75 and 95% reflectance according to the character of their surface.

Grey painted surfaces are difficult to assess; it all depends on what you mean by grey. As little as 5% and as much as 50% can be reflected.

The darkest, most light-absorbent surface is black silk-velvet with a coefficient of only 0·3%, which in practical terms may be taken as zero. Matt-black paint on wood reflects more of the light falling upon it (about 3%) and black paper or board up to 10% which, in fact, would make it look rather more grey than black.

The above figures are necessarily only approximate.

Knowledge of these facts comes in most handy in practice. They tell us, for instance—without the need of experiment—that, when photographing a piece of clean chalk on a sheet of white paper, the chalk will appear white on the photograph, while the paper background—having also appeared to our bare eye as white—is registered as a light grey on the photographic print. We are also informed by comparing the above-mentioned coefficients that—using the same quantity of light—we have to expose a sheet of black paper seven times as long as a sheet of white paper in order to obtain the same density on our negative, or the same effect of brightness on the print.

THE REFRACTION OF LIGHT

Until now we have only considered substances which do not transmit light, but merely absorb and reflect it. But as soon as we go a step further, and consider "transparencies"—glass, Cellophane, celluloid, etc.—we become aware of yet another new phenomenon.

Light is refracted when it enters from one medium of a certain density into a medium of a different density, as from air into glass and *vice versa.* A light-ray falling upon a sheet of glass in the perpendicular is transmitted straight through it without being bent, while every light-ray meeting the surface at an angle other than 90° is deflected from its perpendicular course, the bend becoming more pronounced the more acute the angle of light-incidence. (The angle of refraction is

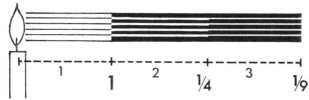

1   2   3

1   ¼   ⅑

The efficacy of illumination is inversely proportional to the square of distance. Two yards away from the light source the efficacy of illumination is one-quarter of that one yard away, and three yards away it is only one-ninth of that one yard away.

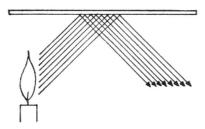

If the reflecting surface is smooth, the reflection will be sharply defined (concentrated, regular, specular reflection). In such a case the angle of incidence will be equal to the angle of reflection.

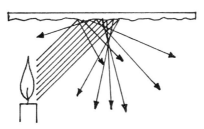

If the reflecting surface is coarse, the reflected beams will not be sharply defined (diffused reflection) and will be dispersed in all directions.

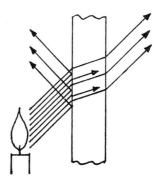

A transparent medium will partly reflect, partly absorb and partly refract the rays of light. The light is refracted, bent, as it enters from one medium of certain density into another medium of different density.

30

further determined by the surface form of the "refractor", *e.g.* a round glass will bend light differently from a plane glass sheet.)

The refracted light-beam after having entered the glass sheet travels straight through it—provided the glass substance is uniform all through—but, in the case of a flat sheet of glass, bends back into the direction of its incidence as soon as it leaves the glass and re-enters the less dense matter of air.

The outstanding application of refraction is, of course, the lens of our camera, which illustrates the fundamental law that, in the case of a transparent object having curved surfaces, light is refracted towards the thickest part of the object—that is to say, towards the centre of a convex lens. Exactly the same effect can be seen through a water-bottle.

A field of photography in which refraction is of the utmost consequence is the photography of glassware. (See p. 182.)

THE COLOUR OF OUR SUBJECTS

So far, we have concerned ourselves only with the colour of transparent substances or with the colour of light itself. In fact, the same basic laws which apply to transparent matter are also applicable to non-transparent (opaque) substances. The only difference is that instead of having to deal with transmission and absorption we now have to deal with reflection and absorption.

We have already seen the way in which opaque substances invariably reflect and absorb light. *A surface therefore appears to us as coloured because it reflects a certain colour, while absorbing others in varying degrees.* Or, in other words, the white light is filtered, this time, however, by reflection, and not as before by transmission.

An object appears to us as red because it reflects only those rays of the incident white light which are red, while it absorbs those which are green and blue. Similarly an object is blue because it reflects blue light rays and absorbs the green, orange, red and, partially, the yellow components contained in the spectrum of the incident light. We describe an object as yellow when it reflects yellow, red and green in different proportions but absorbs blue; we describe it as green when it reflects green, blue-green and yellow but absorbs red, dark blue and violet.

It must now be realised that an object which appears to us as red, blue or green or as any other colour when seen under "white light", will change its colour when illuminated by coloured light. If one goes to the extreme by illuminating a coloured object with its exact complementary colour—for instance, a blue-green dress with red light—the dress will look black. The reason for this is obvious. The filter introduced into the path of the incident white light-beam has absorbed

31

practically all the blue and green rays of the white light, and consequently produces a red light-beam. The blue-green dress can reflect
only blue and green hues. As the incident red light does not contain
any such blue-green hues, the dress is unable to reflect anything at
all, and therefore appears black.

II THE MEANS OF LIGHTING

ELECTRICITY

Since all modern lighting equipment is electrical, the subject of the electric supply and installation deserves, at this stage, a brief prefatory chapter to itself, and this for two reasons.

In the first place, many photographers have little idea of the safe load-carrying capacity of their installation, and one sees cables, switches and fuses overloaded and prevented from becoming dangerous only by the fact that the whole of the lighting equipment is in use for such short periods. Secondly, the average photographer has little idea of the running costs of his lighting units until the bill comes in at the end of the quarter—when it is too late to do anything about it.

The supply company provides current at a stated voltage, and charges for it in units. Most light sources are rated in watts, with the exception of arcs, which, like switches and fuses, are rated in amperes. All these terms are interlinked by the simplest of mathematics.

ELECTRIC UNITS

Let us draw a domestic analogy from the gas supply. The housewife when cooking the Sunday dinner frequently complains of low pressure.

In order to get the dinner ready to time, she has to compensate for this low pressure by turning the taps higher and burning more cubic feet of gas.

These terms of the gas engineer have their corresponding quantities in electricity. The unit of *pressure* is the *volt*, and the unit of *current flow* the *ampere*. The equivalent of the various factors which restrict the flow of gas—the length of pipes, and notably the gas-tap —is *resistance*, measured in *ohms*. While in the gas supply the relationship between the various factors is rather complex, the relationship between the corresponding electrical terms is of the simplest.

By Ohm's law, it can be expressed alternatively as:

$$\frac{volts}{ohms} = amps. \qquad . \quad . \quad . \quad . \quad . \quad 1$$

or—

$$\frac{volts}{amps.} = ohms \qquad . \quad . \quad . \quad . \quad . \quad 2$$

or equally—

$$amps. \times ohms = volts . \qquad . \quad . \quad . \quad . \quad 3$$

Power obviously depends upon both the pressure and the amount of current. Consequently the unit of power, the watt, is equal to the product of pressure and current:

$$watts = volts \times amps. . \qquad . \quad . \quad . \quad . \quad 4$$

or alternatively—

$$amps = \frac{watts}{volts} \qquad . \quad . \quad . \quad . \quad . \quad 5$$

The *unit* by which electricity is charged is based upon the watt, and is equal to a supply of 1000 watts ($= 1$ kilowatt) for 1 hour, or any other similar multiple—for instance, 20 watts for 50 hours, 500 watts for 2 hours, or 2000 watts for $\frac{1}{2}$ hour.

It follows that to ascertain the running cost per hour of any piece of apparatus, such as a lamp, rated in watts, it is necessary only to divide the rated watts into 1000, and multiply by the cost per unit. Thus a 100-watt lamp will run for 1000/100 or 10 hours for one unit; if the cost of current is, say, 3*d.* per unit, then the cost is roughly one-third of a penny per hour. A 250-watt lamp will run for 1000/250 or 4 hours per unit, and, at the same price per unit, will cost $\frac{3}{4}d.$ per hour.

CAPACITY OF INSTALLATION

The load-carrying capacity of any circuit or sub-circuit is always reckoned in amperes. On switches, fuses, and the company's meters one will generally find marked the permissible rating. How is one to ascertain how many lamps of given wattage can be safely run on a circuit rated at so many amperes?

The answer is to be found in equation 5. Thus, supposing it is desired to run, say, five 100-watt lamps and two 250's on a 200-V supply, we first ascertain the total wattage, which equals 1000, and, dividing by 200, we get the answer 5 amperes.

Actually most domestic lighting circuits are rated at 5 amps., but since one would at times need to use other lights—an office light and possibly a dark-room lamp—it would be necessary in this case to have installed a 10-amp. circuit. Such a circuit could carry in addition a 500- or 750-watt electric fire; but a larger fire, of 1 kW or more, might again lead to overloading.

FUSES

What happens when a circuit is overloaded? The cables and switches would overheat, and rapidly lead to danger, but for one safeguard: the fuses. The object of a fuse is to safeguard the rest of the installation, by blowing when the current exceeds that permissible for the installation.

It follows that if a fuse blows, and is replaced, and the replacement blows, the most dangerous thing to do is to put in a heavier fuse. Investigate and discover why the original fuse blew, or, if necessary, call in an electrician; never without expert advice re-wire with a heavier fuse.

Fuses are of two types. For currents up to 10 or 15 amps., ordinary wire fuses are general; if the fuse blows, it is necessary only to open the fuse-box, remove the fuse-carrier (the porcelain bar that pulls out) and insert a new piece of fuse wire *of the same gauge as before.* A distribution box in which there is a number of fuses should have each pair of fuses marked to avoid delay in replacing whichever one has blown.

Heavier fuses are generally of the cartridge type. In all installations the heaviest fuse should be near the meter, and the fuses in the distribution box, or built into the actual lamp-switch, should be lighter, so that if an accident happens and a fuse is blown, it is always the most accessible one.

Always keep at hand a card of 5-amp. fuse wire; naturally, by using it doubled the capacity of the fuse will be increased to 10 amps., so that the same wire can be used for the main fuses, unless they are of the cartridge type.

DIRECT AND ALTERNATING CURRENT

Electric supplies are of two types: *direct* and *alternating*. In the former the current flows always in the one direction—as we conveniently but erroneously say, from the positive pole to the negative. Alternating current, on the other hand, reverses its polarity many times a second. The standard frequency in England is 50 cycles, which means to say that each wire of the circuit becomes successively positive and negative 50 times every second.

Large A.C. installations are generally wired on a three-phase supply. Here we have three wires, coloured generally red, white and green, the current in each of which reverses in polarity at different instants; in addition, there may be a fourth or neutral wire, generally black. The standard voltage in this country is 230 V single-phase or 400 V 3-phase, either, as mentioned, 50 cycles. As we shall see later, three-phase current may be of value in connection with new types of light sources.

Strictly speaking, the five formulae previously given are applicable only to D.C. circuits, and to A.C. lighting and heating circuits. The photographer is, however, unlikely to make use of other plant, except perhaps a small fan motor, and the mysteries of *power factor* need not concern him.

RESISTANCES AND DIMMERS

A *resistance* is merely a length of wire, generally of some special alloy, mounted upon a suitable support, probably in coils, and connected in circuit with a lamp or other apparatus. So far as the photographic studio is concerned, three types of resistances may be used.

The most common is a variable resistance or *dimmer*, the object of which is to reduce the light intensity of a lamp (see p. 42), merely by moving a knob, which puts in circuit a varying length of wire. Another type of resistance permits of running a lamp upon a higher voltage than that for which it is made; thus in a spotlight (see p. 52), it may be preferred to use a 100-V. lamp connected through a suitable resistance to the 200-V or 230-V mains, in order to secure a more concentrated and better defined light spot than is possible with the higher-voltage lamp, with its larger filament. In this case the current (amps.) drawn from the mains is that indicated for the 100-V lamp, and the surplus voltage is simply wasted as heat in the resistance; in the studio this may be undesirable, for which reason resistances are often placed away from the actual lamps.

A third type of resistance is necessary to stabilise an arc lamp (see pp. 43 & 44). This type may also be adjustable, permitting the current through the arc to be varied.

CHOKES AND TRANSFORMERS

Resistances are equally suitable for A.C. or D.C. circuits. But for the former a much more efficient alternative is the *choke* for limiting current, or the *transformer* for reducing voltage. They may be identical in appearance, but differ in that the choke has only two terminals and the transformer four (or occasionally three).

A choke may be used for controlling an arc lamp, while a normal transformer will permit of running our 100-V lamp on the higher mains voltage without the waste of current and unwanted heat of a resistance. Special types of transformers are also obtainable for running arcs, and produce a most efficient unit. Yet another type of transformer is used for stepping-up the voltage for discharge lamps.

PHOTOGRAPHIC LIGHT SOURCES

Only through constant research has science succeeded in emancipating photography from that pitiful state when freckles were a source of worry to the photographer, and a yellow flower a black indelicacy. But at the same time it must be clearly understood that colour consciousness in monochrome photography is, after all, only a question of "reproduction"; it does not give the photographer sufficient power to "create".

It is mainly since the systematic introduction of artificial lighting into photography that the photographer has been able to disentangle himself easily from a timid objectivism, and to lift photography from the status of a purely reproductive medium. It is indeed through the artificial-light source that the photographer now has at his disposal the same mechanical flexibility as any other artist. The fact that photography of today is usually employed for purely utilitarian purposes, or that true artists seem to be still rarer in photography than in other "artistic" professions, must not be taken as proof that the photographic medium as such is still vastly inferior to other media.

Even if we would consider artificial lighting from a purely technical point of view and relate it, not to creative, but purely representational photography, the importance of the artificial-light source—in conjunction with modern negative materials—becomes at once apparent. Obviously the vast majority of the varied problems presented by advertising, commercial or even "big game" camera work could not have been solved before the photographer had the help of electricity.

But all the research put into the construction of photographic lamps is of no avail if the photographer himself does not know why all the work involved was necessary or, in other words, what is the difference between one lamp and another. We therefore have to investigate the problems of artificial-light sources and their fittings in regard to the quality and quantity of light they give out.

QUALITY AND QUANTITY OF LIGHT

The term "quality of light" refers first of all to its actinic properties. *Actinism* is the faculty of light to cause chemical changes. We call one light more actinic than another when it affects the emulsion of the negative in a higher degree. A further question of light quality is whether the light is *soft or hard, direct or indirect*, and, being direct, whether it is *spread or concentrated* (spotted).

The term "quantity of light" refers to the extent of the light output and its bearing on the actual efficiency of the light.

Theoretically, nearly every light source can be used for the production of a photograph. In practice, we can consider as "photographic" only that lighting which has a suitable actinic quality and an intensity which enables us to take our pictures.

Although it is not always necessary, and is even at times undesirable, to work with very short exposures, there must be enough light not to keep our sitter glued to his chair for so long that his expression becomes staring and his whole attitude forced and unnatural. We cannot therefore consider a light source such as a petrol lamp or a candle as "photographic lighting", but merely as possible pictorial assets.

The reason for this becomes still more apparent when we know that a petrol flame is not only of a very limited intensity, but that the composition of its spectrum is also so exaggerated towards red that its actinic value is merely 30% for ordinary negatives, 43% for orthochromatic and approximately 60% for panchromatic materials, compared with the actinic value of a filament lamp of equal intensity.

TYPES OF LIGHT SOURCES

We can divide artificial light sources— as now commonly used in photography—into five main groups: tungsten filament lamps; carbon-arc lamps; tungsten-halogen lamps; electronic flash and flash-bulbs.

For the amateur, tungsten filament lighting is still the easiest to handle for conventional portraiture and still-life photography; although the new, small and lightweight fittings of the effective tungsten-halogen light units will be useful when working under location conditions.

The professional will use all types of light sources according to the demands made upon him by his assignment. Vapour lamps and carbon-arc lighting are hardly ever used nowadays, except for special purposes.

TUNGSTEN-FILAMENT LAMPS

Tungsten filament lamps—also called incandescent filament or half-watt lamps—are hermetically sealed glass bulbs which enclose a

40

thin wire filament. This filament, acting as a resistance, becomes incandescent when electric current is transmitted through it. All modern types, which burn at a high temperature, are filled with inert gas.

The quality of the light emitted from tungsten filament lamps is different from that given out by the sun. It contains *considerably more red rays than sunlight and less blue, violet and ultra-violet rays*. Its effectiveness on ortho-chromatic materials (which are not sensitive to red) is therefore lower than its effectiveness on panchromatic emulsions.

We have also seen that if we wish to get rid of the superfluous influence of violet-blue light-rays, we employ a yellow filter. The yellow light emitted from incandescent filament lamps acts on *orthochromatic* emulsions somewhat like a yellow filter, as the amount of the blue-violet rays contained in this kind of light is considerably reduced in comparison with sunlight.

On the other hand, the large red content of the half-watt light makes lips too bright—this applies especially when the lips have not been made up with dark-red lipstick—and blue eyes too dark when *panchromatic* negatives are used.

The spectral composition of tungsten filament light can easily be altered by "over-running" or "under-running" the bulb. This means *the higher the temperature to which the filament is heated the bluer the light, the lower the temperature of the filament the redder the light will be.* Such alterations of the spectral composition of the light not only influence the actinic energy of the light and the tonal monochromatic rendering of colour but also have the most drastic influence on colour reproduction by colour photography.

For example, if we burn an electric bulb rated at 1000 watts on 200 volts with an increased energy of 240 volts (*i.e.* an increase of 20%), we shall achieve the equivalent luminous intensity not only of a 1200-watt bulb, but also the actinic effectiveness of one of approximately 2000 watts. On the other hand if we burn the same bulb (1000 watts) on 160 volts instead of the rated 200 volts, the actinic effectiveness produced is only equal to that produced by a 500-watt lamp.

Regarding true colour reproduction, we must remember that an increase in temperature increases the blue and a decrease in temperature increases the red content of the light—in other words affects the colour temperature (see page 20).

Every electric filament, however, is constructed to work on a certain voltage; it is therefore obvious that the "*over-running*" *of a lamp*—i.e., *its burning at higher voltage than that stated on it*—*shortens its life considerably*. Now, special photographic bulbs are already over-run when working at the stated voltage, which explains why their life is much shorter than that of ordinary bulbs.

An ordinary electric bulb, as used for domestic purposes, has an expectation of life of approximately 1000 hours when being burnt on the prescribed voltage, a photographic bulb which is rated at 64 volts and burns at 110 volts has a life of only 2 hours. It is, of course, just this high over-running which makes the photo-flood bulb so very efficient, its intensity being not far less than that of an ordinary 1000-watt bulb running on its prescribed voltage. Other photographic lamps may be less over-run and their life correspondingly longer. But one should always be most careful in over-running the already over-run photographic lamps to a further extent.

For the professional photographer it is advisable to have a dimmer (see p. 37) in the studio which enables him to under-run his expensive photographic lamps during the preliminary work of posing his model or arranging a still-life composition. This under-running will therefore make his lamps last considerably longer.

The "character" of the light propagated from an incandescent filament lamp depends on the construction of the filament. *The smaller the light source—i.e. the more compact the filament—the harder is the light and the edges of the shadows cast by it.* The larger the light source —*i.e.* the more extended the filament—the softer is the light produced by it. It is for this reason that our domestic lamps have extended filaments of a somewhat circular construction. Projector-bulbs, burning in special reflectors or spot-light fittings, aim at a hard "effect" lighting and at well-defined shadow images; this is why they have filaments which are condensed in size so far as is practically possible.

The possibility of changing the "character" of light, by using different types of filaments, is one of the great advantages of tungsten filament lamps. Other artificial light sources are not so flexible in this respect.

With all filament lamps, the light emission decreases as the lamp ages. When a bulb blackens it is time to discard the lamp, even though the filament may appear quite sound. In colour photography, the ageing and blackening of the lamp has a serious effect on the true colour rendering.

When purchasing renewals, make sure that the cap is of the right type for the fitting. Lamps of under 250 watts usually have bayonet caps. Most modern spotlight fittings are now of bi-post or giant bi-post types, while the larger flood fittings take either Edison or giant Edison screw bulbs.

INTEGRAL REFLECTOR LAMPS

The integral reflector or sealed-beam lamp is a mushroom-shaped glass envelope internally silvered and with a front face either lightly frosted or moulded to give a fresnel lens effect. It contains a tungsten filament which may be photoflood photopearl (3200° K) or a general-purpose wattage. Such light bulbs provide a complete throw-away lighting unit—a plain lampholder is the only additional equipment required.

The character of light issued varies with the type of front face, and ranges from hard non-focusing spotlighting to moderately diffuse floodlighting. An integral reflector lamp is generally smaller than an equivalent combination lamp plus lighting unit. It may seem cheaper for occasional work as no capital outlay on lighting units is necessary but heavy users will find these lamps prohibitively expensive, as they cost more than a similar standard bulb used in a separate lighting unit.

TUNGSTEN–HALOGEN LAMPS

It has already been pointed out that all tungsten filaments are more efficient when working at high temperature. Unfortunately this is accompanied by rapid evaporation of the filament, so that in a conventionally constructed light bulb lamp life becomes very short. Making the glass envelope as large as possible offers the evaporated metal a larger surface on which to be deposited; this reduces some of the light loss by bulb blackening but cannot overcome the fact that the filament progressively grows thinner and finally breaks.

However, research has shown that if a halogen such as iodine vapour is present in the lamp this combines with the evaporated tungsten, which is then attracted to the *hottest* local surface, *i.e.* the filament. The iodine thus creates a regeneration cycle which greatly increases filament life and elimates bulb blackening.

The cycle is most efficient if the wall of the envelope is close to the filament. The filament is therefore sealed in a narrow tube often made of quartz (this material has a higher melting temperature than glass) and with electrical connections at each end.

Tungsten–halogen (sometimes called quartz–iodine) lamps are compact, highly efficient yet with a life of some 30 hours, and available in a range of wattages. Most lamps of this type burn at a colour temperature of 3400° K. It is most important to remember when fitting these lamps, that the quartz surface should not be touched with the fingers—the grease traces deposited and burnt into the glass when heated may cause fractures.

CARBON-ARC LIGHTING

The name carbon-arc lighting describes aptly its method of working. Electric current flows through two "sticks" of carbon; when these carbons touch they strike a spark in the shape of an arc, thus causing the carbons to burn off at a very high temperature.

Carbon-arc lamps must be burnt through a suitable resistance (see pages 36/37); preferably adjustable, or from a special type of choke or reactive transformer; an ordinary lighting transformer will *not* serve.

Today, carbon-arc lighting is hardly used by the studio photographer although the carbon-arc spotlight produces precise, well-defined shadows and shadow patterns unrivalled by any other light-source. On the other hand, the very hard light quality imposes strong limitation on good modelling, especially if the light must be used in the available space of the smaller commercial studio.

In the film studios high-intensity arc lamps are still widely used in connection with various filters. These vary according to film-stock and other light sources used in the production of colour motion pictures in the studio and out-of-doors.

ELECTRONIC FLASH

If a high voltage capacitor is discharged through an appropriate gas-filled tube a brilliant short-duration flash can be produced. This principle provides us with one of the most valuable forms of studio lighting—*electronic flash*.

Contemporary flash tubes contain xenon gas, giving an almost continuous spectrum close to that of daylight. The tube may be made in any shape: horseshoe to fit within a compact reflector; in the form of a ring to fit around the camera lens and give shadowless lighting; in a spiral leaving a central space for a tungsten modelling lamp and in various compact forms for small units.

The duration and level of illumination of the flash are principally controlled by the nature of the power pack. With small portable units this may only contain batteries or a small accumulator feeding a capacitor which discharges through a low voltage tube *via* a firing switch. More powerful studio units draw electricity from the mains and, through a sequence of rectifier and transformer, store high voltages in banks of capacitors. This energy is released to the tube or tubes *via* a separate low-voltage trigger circuit containing a firing switch.

The light output of electronic flash sets is quoted in joules (each joule is broadly equivalent to the photographic effect of one watt burning for one second). Portable units are available in 100–1000 joules, whilst studio units are built for 6000 joules or more.

When two or three flash tubes are connected to the same power pack the output in joules is normally shared equally between them.

44

The duration of the flash is influenced by the voltage of the pack and type of gas used. General purpose electronic flash varies from about 1/100th sec. for small units, to 1/1000th sec. for large studio units. Shorter duration outfits are available for high speed work in monochrome, but are unsuitable for colour owing to reciprocity failure.

The most useful studio units contain low powered—*i.e.* 100 watt tungsten lamps in each flash head connected to a separate mains circuit. (Some units have a system of "pulsing" the flash tube itself at low power, giving apparently continuous illumination). Such modelling lamps allow us to check the position of shadows and lighting distribution, before actually taking the photograph by flash.

The most common way to fire the flash is *via* connections to switch contacts in the camera shutter. As the flash is virtually instantaneous these contacts are arranged to close at the moment the shutter blades are fully open (X synchronisation). Several separate electronic flash units may be fired in synchronisation simply by connecting one to the camera shutter; photo-electric cells on each of the other packs will fire their particular pack on receipt of light from the camera flash.

Electronic flash lighting may prove costly in initial outlay, but as tubes last for tens of thousands of flashes running costs are very low. It offers special advantages for studio portraiture and fashion photography in both black and white and colour in terms of "freezing" subject movement. Unfortunately, flash tubes are not sufficiently close to the point source requirements of a spotlight system to allow the design of really efficient flash spotlights and cannot as yet offer the flexibility of lighting control obtained from a range of tungsten lamp units.

For the professional a polaroid camera may be useful for an instantaneous check on the lighting set-up and exposure times although flash units are commonly fitted with tungsten guide lamps and flash exposure meters are available.

FLASH-BULBS

Expendable flash-bulbs are entirely different in principle to the photographic light sources previously discussed. Their light is produced by "pyrotechnic" means, *i.e.* the rapid burning of zirconium or magnesium/aluminium wire. Electricity is required only as a means of igniting the metal.

The modern flash-bulb consists of a glass envelope filled with a mass of fine wire in an atmosphere of oxygen. Protruding into the centre of this mass from the base of the envelope are two wires with ends coated in explosive paste. They are spanned by a thin wire filament. In the case of small "capless" bulbs the lower ends of the

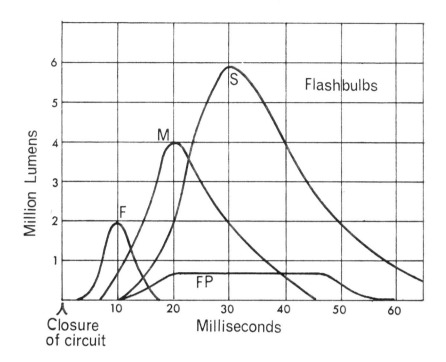

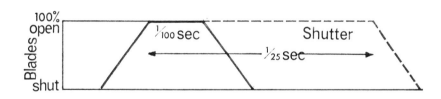

Flash curves for typical fast (F), medium (M), and slow (S) peaking bulbs; also a focal plane (FP) bulb. Below: The Action of a between-lens shutter (set on M synchronisation) shown on the same time-scale. Speeds of ⅒ sec. or slower are essential with S class bulbs.

wire extend down out of the actual glass envelope. Larger bulbs have conventional bayonet or screw caps.

When electricity (a minimum of 3 volts) is applied to the contacts the thin filament glows and burns out, igniting the explosive paste. This throws burning particles into the wire filling which in turn burns out in a brilliant flash.

The time taken between application of electricity and the flash-bulb reaching peak light output varies with the size and design of bulb. Midget bulbs (F or fast peaking) have a delay of 10–12 milliseconds or thousandths of a second. Small capless bulbs and E.S. bulbs of M or medium peaking characteristics take 20 milliseconds to peak, whilst large E.S. bulbs are known as S or slow peaking and take 30 milliseconds. The effective duration of the flash of light is between 1/100th sec. (small F bulbs) and 1/25th sec. (type S).

Flash-bulbs offer very powerful sources of illumination for their size. Normally burning at a colour temperature of 3800°K they are also available with a coating of blue dye, giving an effective colour temperature of 6000° K for balancing with daylight. In the smaller sizes, only the blue-coated type is now generally available.

The power supply for expendable flash-bulbs is far more simple and inexpensive than the power pack for electronic flash. The basic need is simply a circuit containing a 3-volt battery and switch. However, the direct use of batteries for firing tends to lead to unreliability if several bulbs are to be fired over long lengths of cable, or the batteries are less than fresh.

Commercial flash guns contain a circuit in which a small capacitor is charged by the battery, and it is this which fires the bulb when the firing switch is closed. In such a circuit the capacitor may take longer to charge as the battery grows weaker, but discharges full power to the bulb each time. A firing box can also be constructed to offer a number of sockets for the insertion of leads to flash-bulb holders. A further lead connects the switch circuit in the box to the camera shutter.

Synchronisation of the shutter blade's open period with the flash-bulb's peak light output is more difficult in view of the inherent delay in bulb ignition. Most between-lens shutters have an internal delaying arrangement whereby flash firing contacts are closed some 16 milliseconds before the blades are fully open. A selection switch allows either the X (electronic) or M (M class flash-bulbs) circuit to be used.

The character of lighting provided by a small "bare" flash-bulb is close to a point source and can even provide a source for a spotlight.

Warnings: It is dangerous to fire flash-bulbs which, owing to damage, contain oxygen plus air. This mixture may occur if the bulb has received a slight crack; it can result in a violent explosion. Manufacturers usually locate a spot of a "detector" chemical within the

47

bulb, which changes colour in the event of a leakage. Check before using each bulb. Flash-bulbs should not be fired by mains voltage electrically unless designed for this purpose (fused). Bulbs must not be used where there is any risk of igniting inflammable vapour, *e.g.* garages, distilleries, chemical plants and mines.

ELECTRONIC FLASH AND EXPENDABLE FLASH COMPARED

The character of the lighting produced by both flash sources is influenced by reflectors in a similar manner to tungsten sources. The shape of the flash tube may range from a tight spiral approaching the characteristics of a small frosted bulb, to a ring placed around the lens which offers total overall diffusion similar to an overcast sky. Tubes are available in single, straight lengths up to four or five feet long. Placed vertically they produce "hard" compact source illumination over horizontal planes of the subject and diffuse illumination over vertical planes.

The character of flash-bulb lighting becomes more diffuse the more powerful (*i.e.* larger) the bulb in use. The smallest sizes of bulbs are such that it is possible to approximate more closely a point source than with most tungsten units.

In terms of exposure duration the briefer flash from electronic units may effectively "freeze" motion for easy visual analysis. It cannot easily imply motion by the usual symbol of blur; but if such effects are required the slower (1/50th–1/25th sec.) bulb flash offers advantages.

In practical terms other differences between these sources are: electronic flash equipment is more costly, delicate and heavy (relative to power). Modelling lamps found in larger studio units reduce lighting guesswork. Additional electronic heads dilute the power per head unless additional packs are used. Flashbulbs call for less capital outlay but cost more per flash. Delay is caused by the need to change bulbs between pictures, and large numbers of bulbs are bulky to carry. All bulb equipment is independent of mains electricity; various colour temperatures can be employed by changing bulbs; and very high illumination levels are attained by grouped use of bulbs.

Generally electronic flash finds its home in the advertising, fashion or portraiture studio. Expendable flash is most valuable for location, commercial or industrial photography and lighting large architectural interiors.

LIGHTING UNITS

It is in the nature of light to spread out from its source in all directions. The photographer has no use for this wealth of radiated energy; he must subordinate it to his purpose, must subjugate it to his intentions.

The obvious way to bar the haphazard flow of light and to guide it into one direction is to "fence" it in by means of a *reflector*. Thus, these light-rays which radiate backwards and sideways are caught and reflected into one forward stream of light.

REFLECTORS

The extent of control exercised on the direction of light depends on the construction of the reflector, but it is not sufficient merely to force light into a given channel. The photographer must also be able to control its character—that means to influence the extent of its diffusion.

We have already seen that the character of light depends largely on the size of its source; we know that the smaller the light source the harder the light, the larger the light source the softer the light produced by it. By means of adequate fittings the character of light can be still further moulded.

It now becomes apparent that light-fittings have three main tasks to perform: *Firstly* to "round up" light and to lead it into one direction; *secondly* as a consequence of its first task to intensify the light-output; *thirdly* to control the character of light.

To fulfil these various purposes two main groups of photographic fittings have been constructed: *flood-lights* and *spot-lights.*

Generally, these perform two very different functions, arising largely from their different construction and characteristics. The reflector has its more important applications for the floodlight. The spotlight is a focusing lamp using condenser lenses to vary the coverage of its beam.

D

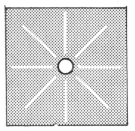

A small bulb (*left*) produces less diffusion than a large bulb (*centre*). A clear glass bulb (*centre*) produces less diffusion than a frosted bulb (*right*). Both these rules apply whether the bulb is for use with or without a reflector.

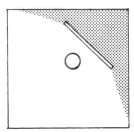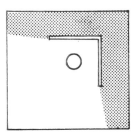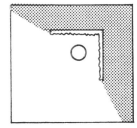

A plain reflector (*left*) produces radical diffusion and directs the light very inefficiently. Conical reflectors (*centre* and *right*) direct the light better, but still give very diffused results. If the reflecting surface is smooth and polished (*centre*), there will be less diffusion than if the finish is dull and rough (*right*). This rule applies to reflectors of any shape. (In this and the other sketches, the amount of white is intended to indicate diffusion, not width of beam.)

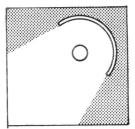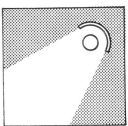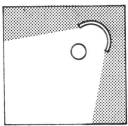

Large reflectors (*left*) produce more diffusion than small ones (*centre*). This again applies to reflectors of any shape, not only to spherical ones as shown above. If the lamp is moved from the focal point (*right*) the amount of diffusion will again be different.

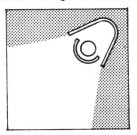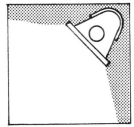

Parabolic reflectors produce less diffused, more concentrated light than spherical or conica ones. More diffusion can be obtained by shielding the bulb (*centre*) or even more by placing a diffusing screen in front of the whole reflector (*right*). This additional means of diffusion can naturally be applied to any shape of reflector.

50

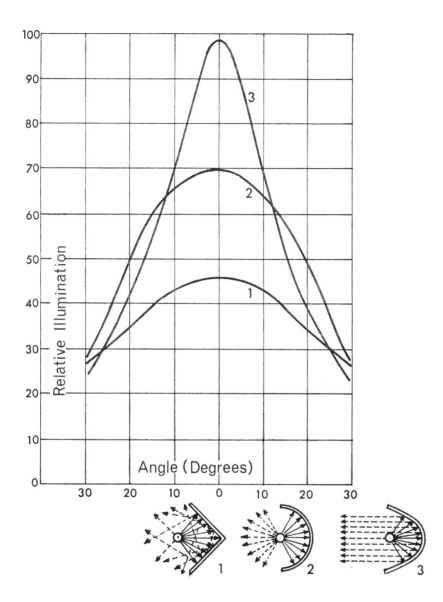

Typical curves showing the relative distribution of light produced by a conical (*1*), spherica (*2*), and parabolic (*3*) reflector, using the same light source. The parabolic (*3*) and spherical (*2*) reflectors compared here have both highly polished metal surfaces, while the conical reflector shown is a cardboard one. It is clearly shown that the relative illumination of the parabolic reflector (*3*) is the highest, but falls off rapidly towards the edges. The spherical reflector produces a more evenly distributed, softer light, but gives relatively less illumination. The conical reflector (*1*) leads to very diffused light and appears the least economic.

51

FLOOD-LIGHTS

As the name implies, *flood-lights aim at broad effects*—at an illumination of a wide area, flooding it all over with an equal intensity. It is typical of flood-lighting that *outside its field of coverage it slowly deteriorates in luminosity, thus creating a range of half-tones which become gradually darker as they recede from the main area of illumination.*

The shape of the reflector and the position of the lamp therein determine the extent of the area illuminated and also the quality of the light itself. *Wide, spheric reflectors give a wider and softer beam of light, while deep, parabolic reflectors produce a harder and more concentrated light.*

Another factor determining the character of the light is the kind of surface inside the reflector. *A dull metal finish naturally produces a more diffused light than a polished surface.* The hardest flood effects are obtained by mirror reflectors.

As already mentioned, *the position of the lamp will affect the angle of beam as well.* In the case of a parabolic mirror, moving the lamp inwards from the focal point will widen the beam; moving it forwards will narrow the beam until a point is reached where the rays cross over, when the beam commences to spread, and the efficiency falls off. In the case of a spherical mirror, any movement of the lamp from the focal point will widen the beam.

In the case of a matt reflector, the size of the reflector has a greater influence upon the softness of the beam. Obviously a *large reflector will represent a larger apparent light source than a small reflector*, and will therefore produce a more diffused illumination.

The extent of diffusion can be further controlled by the choice of bulb used, in conjunction with the reflector. *A clear glass lamp of the projector-type will give the hardest, a frosted bulb with extended filament the softest results.*

Strong diffusion is obtained by cutting off all rays directly propagated by the bulb, by fixing a "shield" in front of the bulb, thus making use of reflected light-rays only.

Still more drastic diffusion is achieved by placing a piece of thin muslin or gauze over the front of the reflector or a sheet of frosted glass between light source and object.

Flood-lighting is either produced by single units or by specially designed aggregates, these finding application on "big sets" where really wide areas have to be evenly illuminated.

SPOT-LIGHTS

Spot-lights aim at producing a "spot" of light. This does not mean that this "spot" must necessarily be small; it is, however, implied

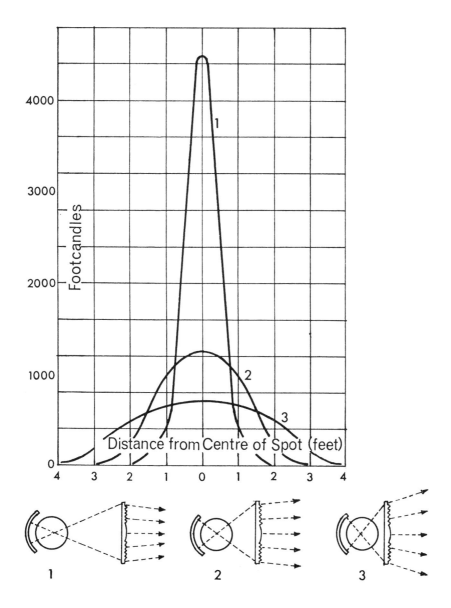

Spot-lights produce light-beams of different widths, and consequently light spots of different diameter as well as intensity, according to the relative positions of the lamp source (the lamp and the mirror behind it) and the condenser. By moving the light source farther away from the condenser (*1*) a converging light beam is produced and consequently a spot of very small diameter but of highest light intensity. The nearer the light source to the condenser lens (*2* and *3*) the wider the beam becomes, the larger the spot and the lower the light intensity.

that a *spot-light produces an accurate light—a sharply defined, spot-like area.* The cinematographer aptly designates the modern spot-light as "precision" lighting.

We have seen that flood-lighting deteriorates outside the illumination area proper—with a slow centrifugal progression. *The light area created by spot-lighting breaks off abruptly, so that light and dark stand side by side without a wide belt of intermediary half-tones between them.* (Some types of spot-lights do produce a *small* half-tone ring around the light-periphery which, however, is so narrow that it is perceived merely as a soft edge, not as an area.)

Spot-light lamps are designed on completely different lines from flood-light lamps. While flood-lights "curb" light by capturing it by means of reflectors, spot-lights have the task of collecting and redistributing it as a beam by means of a lens which is placed in front of the light source, working in conjunction with a mirror behind the light source.

By moving the light source either nearer to or farther away from the condenser lens, one is able to alter the width of the light-beam and, consequently, also the diameter of the spot light. The nearer the light source is moved to the lens the larger will be the light-spot's diameter, the farther away the light source is from the lens the smaller will it be. (See p. 53.)

Compared to flood-lighting, spot-lighting is a hard light and produces clearer shadows and stronger contrasts. Its main purpose, therefore, is not to "flood" but to "accentuate"; or in other words, to produce either a distinct light and shadow pattern or brilliant highlight effects.

This does not mean that spot-lights should never be used as flood units. Indeed, when working on location, such as in an industrial plant, the opposite is true. The focusing facility of spot-lights enables us to "throw" light over far greater distances than flood units can do and enables us to illuminate details in shadow areas which could never be reached by conventional flood-lighting.

By using individual spot-lights of different strengths (from 500 watt to 5 kilowatt each, from well outside the picture area, a very well-balanced lighting scheme can be achieved without the use of any flood units and without losing modelling power and image quality. If necessary, diffusers can be used in front of some of the spot-light units.

However, in the confines of the photographic studio the use of spot-lights should be restricted to their normal function.

The simplest form of spot-light is that fitted with a plan-convex lens, which is flat on one side and convex on the other, the flat side facing the light source. The light-rays transmitted through this lens are refracted according to the laws of optics.

54

Filament spot-lights fitted with primitive condenser lenses have several faults. They not only project the lamp-filament when in focus, but they also show colour aberrations. To eliminate these faults, and also to avoid the excessive thickness of a short-focus lens (with its consequently increased risk of breakage due to heat), spot-light lenses are often used, especially in the larger sizes, in which prismatic rings appear to have been cut. What has actually been done is to step concentric areas of the lens inwards, and at the same time modify the curvature of the outer sections, producing a far more even light area while retaining a sharply defined spot-light effect.

The diameter of the spot can also be controlled by means of an iris. This is obviously inefficient from the point of view of waste of light, but on the other hand permits of producing extremely hard edges when desired.

The qualities typical of spot-lighting, *i.e. hard lighting, good definition of light and shadow edges and stringent light control, are produced at their best by carbon-arc spot-lights.*

FLOOD- AND SPOT-LIGHTS COMPARED

By means of fittings we can control the direction and the quality of light.

Flood-lights direct light into one main direction in a broad manner. The extent of the area of illumination can only be *roughly* influenced by choice of different reflectors and by the distance between the lamp and the area of illumination. It is obvious that (quite apart from the action of the light-fittings) the nearer a lamp is to a background the smaller but more luminous becomes the area of illumination. The light sources suitable for flood-lighting are filament lamps. Flood-lighting is most usually employed for creating a general lighting on which to build up highlight effects or which serves to lighten deep shadows.

Spot-lights, on the other hand, do not merely control the general direction of light, but also enable us to regulate most accurately the extent of the illuminated area. The intensity of the light weakens as the light-rays diverge, and strengthens as they converge. The size of the area of illumination here depends not only on the distance between lamp and background and the size of the lamp-fitting, but also on the focal length of the condenser lens.

The normal light source of spot-lighting is a filament lamp of the projector type. It is important that the broadside of the filament stands parallel to the lens, particularly when bayonet-type bulb sockets are used. Generally spot-lights are now fitted with Bi-Post sockets which naturally keep the bulb securely in the right position.

Most types of projector lamps must be burned at certain angles, specified by the manufacturer: exaggerated tilts up or down will lead to a premature sagging of the filament and to melting the glass envelope, producing a bulge in the glass.

There are, however, spot-light bulbs available which can be used at nearly every angle although these do not produce the same superb light quality of the Type A bulbs normally used.

Recently, specially designed quartz–iodine light sources have been produced for use in 2-kW spot-light fittings. These have the advantage that the light quality will remain constant and not deteriorate with use, an important consideration in colour photography. On the other hand, this new light source has the grave disadvantage that it will give a "double image" when the spot-light is in the "spotted" position.

Flood-lighting as well as spot-lighting can be diffused (softened) at will by either fabric or glass "diffusers". Leaving this fact out of account, we can classify light sources and fittings in their "light-quality" as shown on p. 50.

THE "COLORTRAN" LIGHTING SYSTEM

Although this system was originally produced for cinematography work, still photographers find it increasingly useful for colour and monochrome work on location. As these light-fittings use integral reflector lamps, different types can be chosen to give a mixed bag of lighting units, producing spot, hard flood and soft flood effects. The lamp-stands are collapsible and very light. At the present time, bulbs are obtainable in two main groups.:

The first consists of three lamp types which all emit a hard to medium-hard light quality. One type gives a narrow angle, spot effect; another medium and the third a wide angle light emission. I, personally, find the spot-effect lamp least useful; it cannot be focused and the light quality cannot be compared with that of a conventional spot-light.

The second group of bulbs produces a soft light suitable as fill-in floods or to give an even, general, illumination. These lamps are produced in three types at 500, 1000 and 1500 watts.

We know that most damage to the filament of an incandescent lamp takes place when it is being switched on from cold. So if a lamp is switched on at a reduced "warm-up" voltage the lamp life is greatly extended because the filament acquires a substantial resistance before the voltage is stepped up to full power.

By the same principle, an excess voltage applied during the short period whilst a photograph is actually taken allows a much higher

56

illumination level without appreciable reduction in lamp life if pre-warming has taken place.

The Colortran system consists of a multi-tapped transformer. This is connected between 250-volt mains and up to six or so integral reflector 120-volt lamps of various wattages. On the transformer a rotary contactor is provided for each lamp, enabling the lamp to be be brought up in stages from "preheating" voltage to the excess voltage necessary for 3200° K or 3450° K. A meter on the transformer indicates colour temperature at each stage. With such a system lamps, stands, cables, etc., can be lightweight and extremely portable. Illumination levels normally associated with bulky lighting equipment of conventional pattern are possible *for the short period this is actually needed.* For example, a Colortran lamp using 900 watts at the highest tapping gives the same light as a standard 5000-watt lamp.

INDIRECT LIGHTING

Besides the light sources already discussed, the photographer can also employ means of indirect lighting, *i.e.* using light only after it has been intercepted by a reflective surface and redistributed by it. When working with artificial lighting it is best to employ matt white surfaces which can reflect up to 90% of the incident light and produce very soft highlights, diffused shadow forms and good modelling. It is unfortunate that in common usage the term reflector is used to describe two different things, a light fitting and just a light-reflecting surface. For indirect lighting a reflector can be anything from a sheet of white cardboard to a large movable white screen or the special white umbrella reflectors. The last are used particularly in conjunction with electronic flash. In recent years diffused indirect lighting has been used increasingly in portraiture, fashion and certain types of advertising photography. This low-contrast lighting is particularly useful in colour photography where excess of contrast is often undesirable. In monochrome photography, however, soft indirect lighting should be used for special effects and not as a simple way out of the complexities of direct studio lighting.

Different, stronger effects are obtained by indirect lighting when reflectors consisting of *matt silver-paper* are used and we can achieve vigorous highlight effects by employing a *mirror* as reflector. *Shiny silver-paper* reflectors are not to be recommended, as they produce scattered and irregular reflections which are difficult to control. Indirect light sources are invaluable for the rendering of purely reflective objects, like silver, etc.

A factor that must not be overlooked when we are striving for low-key or contrasty effects is the reflection and diffusion of light due to the walls of the room. In a large studio this may be relatively unimportant, but *in a small room with light walls, the repeated reflections may make it impossible to secure dark shadows.*

To overcome such difficulties, the ciné-cameraman makes use of sheets of black material on wire frames in order to shield stray light from the lamp as required. Alternatively, there are movable metal shields or flaps, called "barn doors", which can be attached to individual lamp fittings to give a similar effect.

Similarly, small screens of lightproof or slightly translucent material cut out to circular or other curved shapes can be fixed on a swivelling rod attached to a standard to cut off areas of direct or reflected light and create small fields of shadow on the subject.

LIGHTING OUTFIT FOR STUDIO AND HOME

Let us now try to form some idea as to the kind and the number of light-fittings required by amateur and professional photographers in consideration of the various tasks they might wish to perform.

The size of a light-fitting depends primarily on the size of the light source; the size of the light source depends on the power of its light-output. Generally speaking the higher the wattage of a bulb the larger the reflector required. Thus, the choice of light-fittings must be subordinated to the individual photographer's practical requirements.

The amateur, therefore, working at home tackling only small "sets" and not aiming at the highest possible shutter speeds, will not inconvenience himself with the large and expensive professional fittings.

The professional photographer, on the other hand, must carefully consider the number and kinds of lamps he is going to buy. It is obvious that he will also have to consider his purse, but the decisive factor for his choice is governed by his requirements. It will not do to try to save money by buying a few small fittings and then attempt to tackle pictorial problems which can only be solved by an expensive and efficient lighting equipment.

For the *amateur with humble intentions* three reflectors fitted with photographic bulbs are adequate. They serve the purpose of taking the wife and the kiddies.

The *ambitious amateur* who wants to try his hand on proper portrait-studies or still-life pictures should acquire a more professional outfit. One small spot-light fitted with a 500-watt projector lamp and two or three flood-reflectors fitted with 250- or 500-watt filament lamps are recommended. If a 500-watt spot-light seems an excessive expenditure, smaller spot-lights are now available which take a 200-watt

58

projector bulb. These small spot-lights, considering their low wattage, are highly efficient; but the flood-lighting needs to be limited in accordance by using either stronger diffusion or filament lamps not exceeding approximately 250 watts each.

Under no circumstances can flood aggregates be recommended to the amateur. These flood units, which consist of two or three flood reflectors mounted on a single stand, cast three different shadows and also give three separate highlights in the eyes. Even the amateur cinematographer, who needs a great quantity of light, will find one single high-powered flood unit preferable to these difficult to manage and unnecessarily cumbersome aggregates.

To determine the *professional* photographer's needs in regard to lighting equipment is not so easy. Keeping in mind that we have two different aspects to take into account, the photographer's scope and his method of working, and that we have to allow for slight adjustments because of personal preferences, I believe that the following suggestions will give quite a good idea of reasonable requirements within a highly competitive profession.

LIGHTING EQUIPMENT FOR THE PORTRAIT PHOTOGRAPHER

(a) *Incandescent Lighting* Techniques
   4 500-W floods
   2 1000-W spot-lights
   Diffusers and reflector boards

Consumption: on 240 V: 4 kW = approx. 17 amps.

(b) *Electronic Flash Lighting* Techniques
   1200 joules electronic flash power pack with up to 4 heads, equipped with white-lined umbrella reflectors

Consumption: on 240/250 V A.C. 13 amps. whilst charging only

LIGHTING EQUIPMENT FOR THE COMMERCIAL PHOTOGRAPHER SPECIALISING IN STILL-LIFE WORK

Incandescent Lighting only

   1 1000-W spot-light
   1 500-W spot-light
   1 500-W spot-light suspended on boom
   Snouts (cone) of different apertures for the above
   1 200-W "dinky" spot-light
   2 500-W floods
   Diffusers and reflector boards

Consumption on 240 V: 3200 watts—approx. $15\frac{1}{2}$ amps.

LIGHTING EQUIPMENT FOR THE ADVERTISING PHOTOGRAPHER

(a) *Incandescent Lighting Techniques*
   4 2-kW spot-lights
   3 500-W spot-lights
   1 500-W overhead spotlight

4-kW flood-light facilities partly in troughs and partly in individual reflectors
Snouts for 500-W spot-light
Barndoors
Reflector screens

Consumption on 240 V: approx. 14 kW = max. 60 amps.

(b) *Electronic Flash Techniques*
    2 5000-joule electronic flash packs
    2 5-ft. strip tubes
    5 coiled tube floods
    1 ring flash head
    Umbrella reflectors

Consumption on 240/250 V A.C. up to 30 amp whilst charging only. (The sophisticated requirements of Consumer Advertising may now necessitate possession of both incandescent and electronic flash equipment.)

LIGHTING EQUIPMENT FOR THE FASHION PHOTOGRAPHER

(a) *Incandescent Lighting Techniques*
    1 2-kW overhead spot-light movable on monorail
    4 2-kW spot-lights on individual floor stands
    4 500-watt spot-lights
    4-kW flood facilities partly in troughs and partly in individual reflectors
    Snouts and barndoors
    Reflector screens

Consumption on 240 V: 16 kW =approx. 67 amps.

(b) *Electronic Flash Techniques*

As for the Advertising Photographer (see above) but the 5000-joule power packs should be capable of "splitting down" into portable 1000–1200-joule location units.

LIGHTING EQUIPMENT
FOR THE ILLUSTRATIVE INDUSTRIAL PHOTOGRAPHER

The demands in industrial photography vary greatly. The following suggestions are therefore broken into two groups to establish a reasonable minimum and a reasonable maximum.

(a) *Minimum lighting set-ups*
    4 2-kW spot-lights
    2 500-W spot-lights   Consumption 240 V
    1 200-W Dinky spot-light   9 kW = approx. 38 amps.
    Distributor boards with cable
    Extension cables OR
    1 Colortran System containing six light units (mixed) OR
    flash-bulb capacitor box capable of reliably firing 20 to 30 bulbs over 200 yards of cable.
    12 single flash-bulb holders with wide-angle reflectors
    20×10 yd. length of connecting cable
    6 stands
    12 clamps
    Adaptors for capless bulbs
(b) *Maximum lighting set-ups* (required for dramatic large-scale treatments)
    2 5-kW spot-lights
    6 2-kW spot-lights
    2 500-W spot-lights

60

1 200-W 'Dinky' spot-light
Barndoors for 5-kW and some of the 2-kW spot-lights
Distributor boards
Extension cables

Consumption: at 240 V = 23 kW = max. 100 amps. (In practice this load will require special arrangement at the location to obtain the necessary power on single phase supply.)

EQUIPPING A STUDIO

If you are equipping a studio for the first time you must realise that the choice of the right kind of lighting equipment is of the utmost importance. Before buying lighting equipment, make up your mind which branch of photography you are going to specialise in and also consider which type of clientele you are going to cater for. If, as a fashion photographer, you will specialise in simple, illustrative treatments such as used for knitting leaflets or mail order catalogues, you will require less ambitious equipment than if you were to serve a highly sophisticated market, the glossy magazines or cosmopolitan advertising agencies. It is important that you first decide on a definite business policy before equipping yourself and do remember that under-equipping can be just as costly as over-equipping.

Not only this. Ask yourself if you are sure that you have found a definite "style" of working. If you have not, it is better to buy, at first, the absolute minimum you need just to carry on, and to supplement your equipment as experience makes you aware of your needs. If, on the other hand, you have a style of your own let this govern your choice.

LAMP-STANDS AND FIXTURES

It is not for us to describe all kinds of lamp-stands and fixtures on the market. The manufacturers' catalogues give ample information about the various types available. At the same time it seems necessary to discuss this matter from the point of view of the practising photographer—amateur or professional.

It is obvious that the construction of a lamp-stand depends to a great extent on the size and weight of the lamp it has to carry. The amateur does not require any heavy and elaborate "tripods", which would only be a nuisance to him.

The importance of keeping our lamp equipment flexible is repeatedly stressed in this book.

The amateur especially, who does not require a huge bank of light for general flood effects, is not justified in hampering his freedom of action by unnecessarily complicated fixtures.

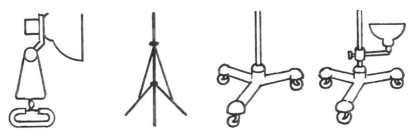

Examples of lamp bases. *From left to right:* (1) Clamp-on unit allows secure attachment to any vertical or horizontal support. (2) Tripods are mostly used in connection with light telescopic stands. (3) The studio base with ball-bearing castors provides the most convenient and most rigid means of positioning. (4) Ball-bearing base with movable low-angle bracket.

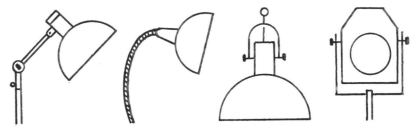

Methods of lamp adjustment. (1) May be clamped at any angle. (2) Provides added flexibility, but is apt to lose its rigidity. (3) and (4) are usual methods of supporting spot-lights and other heavy fittings.

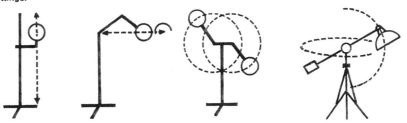

Methods of adjusting light sources. (1) Provides vertical and angular adjustment. (2) Provides lateral adjustment. In (3) the light sources can be adjusted in a variety of positions. If close together a harder light will be produced than if they are separated. (4) Boom-light fitting providing adjustment of lamp for top-lighting as well as under-lighting.

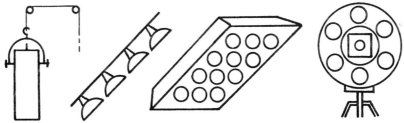

(1), (2) and (3) are three different types of overhead fittings, giving progressively a softer illumination. In (1) the lamp is masked to cover a small area and can be adjusted for height or angle. (4) is a fitting for shadowless lighting, the lamps in a ring reflector surrounding the camera.

For the professional photographer these problems are not so easily solved. Not only has he heavy lamps requiring a sturdy support, but he may also need a light-source which covers a very wide field of illumination. We have to distinguish between two groups of lamp supports—stands and wall or ceiling fixtures.

Lamp-stands should run on large castors and be easily movable; this applies especially when the stand carries a heavy lamp. Another point to be watched is that the lamp can be *elevated to a good height* without *undue effort* and again that it can be *lowered almost to the ground.* To this end one should insist on double telescopic stands instead of the slightly cheaper stands with single extension. This is particularly important if the photographer is called upon to photograph standing figures. For low-angle lighting, lamp-stands with special attachable low-angle brackets are recommended. These low-angle brackets are most useful to the industrial photographer who has to light figures bending down and who uses low-angle lighting for certain dramatic effects comparatively often.

To make transport easier, the photographer who has to work on location away from his studio is strongly advised to choose lamp-stands which, whilst retaining sturdiness, are collapsible at their base.

The average portrait or advertising photographer should restrict himself to separate lamps whenever possible. Studios are too often overloaded with gadgets on ceilings and walls, which—although extremely impressive—prove in practice to be more of a hindrance than a help to creative work. It is only by moving all his lamps wherever he may want them that the photographer can make full use of the many technical and creative possibilities of artificial lighting. Fixed light sources have not only a restricted radius of action; they also induce the photographer to base his ideas on the limited scope of "ready for use" and more or less stable conditions of lighting. It is in this way that imagination becomes sterile and static.

However—let us not generalise, for there are occasions when fixtures are needed. *Studios specialising in photographing of big sets,* groups and elaborate fashion arrangements might be unable to produce the necessary *all-round illumination* without some kind of light source which illuminates the set from a good distance and from a good height. It is for these requirements that *bank-lighting* has been constructed which moves freely along the ceiling by means of steel runners.

Another fixture universally useful is the *overhead spot- or flood-lamp.* In the studio it is best to suspend the lamp from the ceiling allowing for adjustments regarding height and lateral movement. This type of fitting is particularly important for the fashion and general advertising photographer. For the photographer working on location, but also for the portrait and still-life specialist, a light but well-constructed boom-light is a more suitable lamp for direct top-lighting.

Whatever our requirements, whatever our personal inclinations, we should always remember that we must not be bluffed by looks when buying our lamp-stands. A small collapsible flood-tripod, recommendable to the amateur, might often be more practicable than a heavy chromium-plated affair which serves the same purpose. One is too easily tempted to leave many possibilities untried, just because the inconvenience of moving heavy lamps makes the execution of an idea appear far more difficult than it is in reality.

THE ESTIMATION OF EXPOSURE

EXPOSING MONOCHROME MATERIALS

In black-and-white photography, the whole object of photographic lighting is to produce on the negative an exposure which, when printed through to a positive, will reproduce the light and shade of the original subject, not necessarily as they actually existed, but as the aesthetic taste of the photographer dictates.

Exposure is possibly the most controversial subject in the whole realm of photography. To a certain extent one can reduce it to scientific terms—to the reproduction within a given tone range on the negative of the range of light intensities of the subject. But innumerable factors, aesthetic and practical (the latter including the developing of the negative and the making of the print) suggest that any such method can certainly never provide a final dictum.

BRIGHTNESS RANGE AND DEVELOPMENT

Let us dispel once and for all the illusion that incorrect exposure can always be compensated for in development. Certainly, if we have an under-exposed plate, as development proceeds the highlights will gradually increase in contrast; but the shadows will still be clogged. Similarly, if the plate is over-exposed, it may be possible by a very brief development to prevent the highlights burning out, but we shall hardly be able to obtain a satisfactory print. Also it must be remembered that only a moderate degree of over-exposure accentuates the appearance of "grain". Yet the photographer's classic rule that *over-exposure is better than under-exposure* contains some measure of truth. The amateur, however, who patronises the local chemist is liable to find that, in the effort to compensate for the usual run of under-exposed snapshots, a negative that is in the least over-exposed

E

may be developed to a state where the highlights are hopelessly clogged.

The greater the brightness range of a subject, the more accurate must be the exposure. If we have a subject with a small brightness range, the exposure may vary over a range of as much as 10 to 1, and we shall still get a negative which, given suitable development, will produce a satisfactory print, with both highlight and shadow detail. But if we have a subject with a much wider brightness range, the exposure must be precise, and the negative must be developed to give a soft negative all the tones of which can be printed through to the positive.

It will be apparent that when we refer to subject brightness *we do not mean the visual brightness, but the brightness as seen by the photographic emulsion.* Thus to an orthochromatic emulsion a pure red, no matter how brightly lit, could never be over-exposed (although let it be emphasised that few reds, or any other colours, are actually pure!).

It is, however, assumed that for all work with artificial light, panchromatic materials will be used and visual brightness is therefore a fairly safe guide, an exception being when filters are used.

FACTORS DETERMINING EXPOSURE

A number of factors having a direct bearing on the subject of exposure have already been briefly mentioned. Ignoring for the moment aesthetic considerations, let us list these and other practical factors under three headings, those attributable to the subject, those inherent in the negative material and those forming part of subsequent treatment. In each horizontal section are included co-acting factors.

VARIABLE FACTORS AFFECTING EXPOSURE

Subject	Negative Material	Subsequent Treatment
Intensity of Light Brightness of Subject	Speed of Emulsion	Type and Degree of Development
Colour of Light Colour of Subject Colour of Filters	Colour Sensitivity of Emulsion	
Brightness Range of Subject	Latitude of Emulsion	Type and Accuracy of Development

This table takes no account of the vital factor of *lens aperture*, as—apart from the effect upon the depth of field—its influence can be stated precisely.

EXPOSING COLOUR MATERIALS

We have already seen that it is undesirable to manipulate the development of colour materials. In the case of *reversal colour materials* lighting should be so arranged that the brightest important *highlight has no more than ten times the luminosity of the darkest shadow*. Colours outside these limits will probably be desaturated and slightly distorted.

The importance of these limits varies with the type of subject matter. Sunlit landscapes, for example, may offer a subject brightness range of several hundreds to one, but on the final transparency overheavy shadows and "burnt out" highlights may be pictorially acceptable. In the studio a 10:1 brightness range is probably un-necessarily high and means that we are leaving no room at all for exposure error.

Using ratios lower than 10 : 1 may seem to restrict the possibilities of lighting, until it is remembered that, unlike black-and-white photo-graphy, final results depend on *colour contrast* as much as lighting contrast. It may even be possible to produce a satisfactory colour picture with completely flat lighting, provided that the photographer has carefully arranged visual contrast between one hue and another. Lighting and colour contrast are therefore inextricably linked.

The black-and-white photographer commencing reversal colour work in the studio must usually discipline himself to give extra illumination in the shadow areas until a meter reading shows these to be not more than one-eighth or one-fifth of highlight intensity.

Colour negative materials are of lower emulsion contrast than reversal films and of course allow an important manipulation stage in printing. However, even though a wider range of subject brightnesses may be recorded on the negative it may not be possible to accom-modate them on the final printing paper. The range of print grades is for example far more limited in colour. It is therefore wiser to work within the same brightness range restrictions as reversal materials, but remembering that rather greater exposure latitude is possible.

The exact extent of exposure latitude with colour films is impos-sible to quote, depending as it does on emulsion characteristics, subject brightness range, and the purpose of the picture, not to mention the aesthetic intent of the photographer. If a range of exposures is to be given on reversal material these will show appreci-able difference at $\frac{1}{2}$-stop intervals. Remember that it is often more acceptable to *slightly* underexpose a transparency (*i.e.* image darker) if it is intended for reproduction or screening with a powerful pro-jector. Using colour negative film, exposure tests can be more usefully varied by one-stop intervals, with a weighting in favour of slight *over*-exposure rather than under-exposure. Sheet-film users of both types of film must also remember to consult the "batch variation" sheet packed within the box for speed setting corrections. Correction of reciprocity failure may be necessary.

Remember also that any slight extra camera bellows extension which reduces image brightness, perhaps imperceptibly in terms of black-and-white materials, can show unwelcome exposure errors in colour tripacks.

Normal exposure must be multiplied by (linear magnification $+1)^2$

or
$$\frac{\text{Total bellows extension}^2}{\text{Lens focal length}^2}$$

DETERMINATION OF EXPOSURE

In the olden days one was often impressed by the professional photographer who just "took the cap off his lens" to give what seemed to be a somewhat arbitrary exposure. Even today the good Press photographer is rarely seen to use an exposure meter.

We must not be misled by this. These photographers, usually working in monochrome, were, and still are, able to rely on experience based on well-known conditions of lighting, environments and film stock. However, although the experienced professional photographer can still rely on this judgment when working in black-and-white, it is obviously quite impossible to guess at an exposure when photographing in colour.

As matters stand today every photographer should use an exposure meter as a matter of course. Modern film processing methods rarely permit attention being given to individual negatives during development.

The industrial photographer especially, however great his experience, is confronted daily with new problems of exposure estimation. Not only has he to consider the light given by his lamps, but he has to take into account also incidental daylight or the brightness of furnaces, and so on. The photographer operating in works where he cannot help looking directly into the glare of furnaces must never rely on the accuracy of his visual perception. Conditions change too often and too rapidly to make his eyes a reliable exposure meter.

In other words: Guesswork is out.

EXPOSURE METERS

There are different types of exposure meters on the market and it would go too far here to discuss all the different systems. It will suffice if we concentrate on that type of exposure meter which, for the average photographer, is the most suitable from the point of view of practicability and also of expense—the photo-electric meter.

68

This, at first sight, is the simplest to manipulate; it is merely necessary to point the instrument towards the scene (or in some cases towards the light source) and read off the required exposure from a scale. All up-to-date types embody rules for adjusting the exposure to suit different lens apertures and different emulsion speeds.

So far estimation of exposure by means of an up-to-date photo-electric meter seems all too easy. And, indeed, for average subjects with a well-balanced lighting any photo-electric meter will give a reliable reading. If, however, we encounter subjects which are out of the ordinary, particularly those with unequal areas of brilliant high-light and deep shadow, any exposure meter must be used in a very definite manner and with common sense. It is obvious that an exposure meter which has a wide angle of reception will integrate the overall brightness of a scene and take account neither of the brightness range, nor of the fact that either highlight or shadow may be just a small area.

Therefore, if we use a photo-electric meter under difficult conditions, it is essential that we make not only one all-over reading, but several readings of the different parts of the object. Instead of just pointing the exposure meter ahead of us we must take it near to our subject, measure its highlights *and* its shadows, thus determining whether the contrast ratio as such can still be reproduced by a photographic emulsion. If we find that contrast is excessive we shall have either to subdue the highlights or to lighten our shadows to an extent that allows for suitable reproduction of shadow detail without clogging the highlights. Once this is done we have to consider the effect which we intend to obtain. If, for instance, we are after one of those dramatic images which rely for their effect on simplicity and little shadow detail, we must expose on a meter reading obtained from one of our highlight readings. If, however, we want a greater range of half tones reproduced we must allow a more generous exposure time, which has been given to us by a reading from one of our middle tones.

Another factor which must not be overlooked is the subsequent development of our negatives. If we use a fine-grain developer which entails "exposure loss", naturally we have to allow for this in the adjustment of the film speed scale of our exposure meter.

FILTER FACTORS

Almost invariably *the use of a filter involves an increase in exposure* (see p. 18). The amount of increase due to a particular filter is known as the filter factor.

One commonly speaks of a three-times filter or a five-times filter, indicating usually yellow filters needing three or five times the normal exposure. But actually it is impossible to consider filter factor without reference both to the light source and to the emulsion.

Consider the case of a red filter. Used with panchromatic stock in daylight, it will cut the ultra-violet, blue, and green bands—three-quarters of the total available light—and will consequently need about a four-times increase in exposure. On the other hand, used with an orthochromatic stock, it will cut practically all the usuable light rays, and will increase the exposure enormously.

Again, using the same filter with incandescent lighting, it will not cut as much as three-quarters of the light, because such light sources are richer in red emission. Consequently, using panchromatic emulsion, the filter factor may be only about 2. With sodium lighting the filter will probably cut none at all of the light, and the factor will be 1; with mercury lighting it will on the other hand cut probably 90% or more of the light, and the factor will be from 10 to 15.

A filter factor is therefore entirely meaningless unless it is specified as correct for the stock and the illuminant actually used. By comparing the transmission spectrogram of the filter with the sensitivity spectrogram of the emulsion, and bearing in mind the characteristics of the lighting, it is, however, possible to assess the factor with some degree of accuracy, although experiment is of course the safest way.

EXPOSURE ESTIMATION WITH FLASH

The most common method of calculating exposure when using flash is by means of "flash factors" or guide numbers.

This number is produced by multiplying the distance between flash and subject (feet) by the *f*-number required. For example, a flash 5 ft. from subject requires *f*8. Flash factor = 40. Inversely, using a flash with a factor of 110, *f*11 is required at 10 ft. or alternatively *f*16 at approximately 7 ft.

The flash factor itself is determined by the light output of the bulb or tube on the one hand and the speed of the film on the other. It is also influenced by the tones of the subject, the reflective properties of the surroundings, type of reflector behind the flash source, shutter speed (if used at less than 1/25 sec. with bulbs) and intended development conditions.

Some of these variables are eliminated by standardised equipment and technique. Type of reflector for example, standardised development and shutter speeds can all be kept constant.

Using M synchronisation, 1/50 sec. utilises most of the effective light from M type bulbs, but 1/25 sec. is necessary for slower-peaking S bulbs. Most electronic flash is of shorter duration than 1/100 sec. and this shutter speed on X synchronisation uses all the emitted light. Users of focal plane shutter cameras should consult the maker's instructions. With 35-mm. focal plane equipment it is usually possible to use electronic flash at speeds of 1/60 sec. or slower but ordinary bulbs may call for a shutter speed no faster than 1/15 to 1/30 sec. Focal plane bulbs with extended peak duration can be used at the faster shutter speeds. Manufacturers of flash illumination sources and films publish recommended flash factors for particular combinations of bulb and film. These should only be taken as a basis of test under your own working conditions, as the figures usually assume "average", light-toned subjects and surroundings.

When flash-bulbs are used in large reflectors in clusters, the flash factor for a single bulb must be multiplied by the *square root* of the total number of bulbs to obtain the factor for the cluster as a whole. Two bulbs with single factor of 100, for example, combine to give $100 \times 1 \cdot 4 = 140$; three bulbs $100 \times 1 \cdot 7$; four bulbs 100×2, and so on.

When using several bulbs or tubes in separate heads placed around the subject we can calculate exposure by the flash factor of the "key" source only, ignoring the others.

If the flash source is reflected or "bounced" from a diffusing surface the flash factor must be reduced by an amount depending upon the reflective properties of the surface. Bouncing from a typical white plaster ceiling for example, the flash factor should be halved. Beware of bouncing flashlighting from even slightly tinted walls when shooting on colour material. Having established the effective flash factor under bounced lighting conditions the required aperture is found by dividing the factor by the total *flash-to-reflecting surface-to-subject distance.*

It may be necessary to use flash to fill in shadows caused by some other light source as, for example, to reduce the lighting contrast of a portrait backlit by the sun. Let us assume that in this case the flash is used on the camera to avoid creating additional shadows. We can calculate exposure as follows:

Distance from camera (and flash) to subject = 5 ft.
Factor for the particular flash/film/surroundings combination = 60 f-number for correct exposure = f12.
Meter reading for parts of the subject lit by sun = $\frac{1}{35}$ sec. at f12. $\frac{1}{35}$ sec. at f12 would therefore give a 1:1 balance between flash and sunlight. To make this lighting appear more realistic the sun should appear brighter than the flash, say 4:1 ratio. This may be achieved by either:
changing to a smaller flash source, having half the flash factor,
placing a diffuser over the flash, absorbing 75% of the light output,
doubling the distance between flash and subject.

N.B. The chosen ratio between the two sources should take into account the accommodation of the film. For example, if it is to be shot on medium contrast panchromatic film the lighting ratio may prove more effective at 20 : 1. When using colour this ratio might be as low as 2 : 1, and the flash source must of course match the daylight in colour temperature.

ELECTRONIC FLASH IN THE STUDIO

The popularity of electronic flash for studio photography has given rise to the need for a quicker, more accurate means of exposure estimation than that by flash factors. This has led to the important introduction of the electronic flash meter which provides the most accurate, if expensive, method for professional use.

The flash meter is attached to the firing lead of the flash unit and placed close to the subject, facing the camera. It measures the duration and intensity of the flash by reading the *incident* light and automatically converting it into an exposure reading by merely pressing a button on the meter.

These meters do not only serve the quick estimation of exposure but the easy assessment of lighting balance between different light sources.

If the flash-heads are equipped with tungsten modelling lamps an ordinary exposure meter can be used. The output relationship of modelling lamp and flash tube must first be established, *viz.*:

(1) Heads are set up for photography and a meter reading of the modelling lamp illumination measured from a white card on the subject.

(2) A number of test exposures at possible apertures are made and processed.

(3) The aperture resulting in correct exposure is checked on the meter dial and the shutter speed opposite this *f*-number is noted. The shutter speed now becomes a "datum mark".

When shooting the next subject with flash, stage one is carried out and opposite the shutter speed noted in stage 3 will be found the required aperture for the flash. When changing the film in use the film speed is adjusted on the meter in the normal way.

III THE PRINCIPLES OF LIGHTING

F

There is only one way of learning how to build up photographic lighting—by learning to "see". There is also only one way of learning how to apply this photographic lighting—by learning to feel sensitively and to think intelligently.

Rules *are* essential to guide the students and to acquaint him with the wealth of experiences accumulated by masters of his profession. However, let us once and for all realise that photographic lighting can never be taught *or* learnt by hard-and-fast rules alone.

But one thing the student *can* be taught, namely, how to use light and shadow in order to perform the task which he *himself* has set.

It is only natural that styles vary and we have seen many distinctly different modes of visual expression during the last 30 years. While, for instance, the leading photographers of the late 'thirties and 'forties used dramatic and complex chiaroscuro effects with much impact in portraiture and fashion photography, the trend of the 'sixties is towards softer, sometimes flat images which are based not as much on the intention of creating a heightened awareness of three dimensionality and of detail, but on the desire to create an illusion of activity and action.

The same aim shows in modern industrial photography, but it is interesting that here the development of the visual style (particularly in monochrome) is entirely opposite to that of fashion photography and portraiture. Whilst in the 'thirties industry was photographed nearly exclusively by available light and illustrated in very broad, general terms with a marked absence of activity, the best of industrial photography today portrays industry dramatically in concept and in detail.

All these changes come about not only because of a change of mentality as one generation follows another; they are often engendered or accelerated by new technical devices produced by the photo-

74

graphic manufacturer. The influence of electronic flash upon the attitude to portraiture and fashion is very much apparent, whilst the wider use of controllable artificial lighting on location has led to the present "new look" of industry.

It is most important that both teachers and students of photography realise that in spite of all the periodic changes of styles and fashions, the systematic discipline of fully investigating *and* applying the whole complex range of lighting effects must be taught and absorbed during the early years of a photographer's development. To pick up one's lighting by rule of thumb is not enough.

Lighting must not be reduced to a mere means of illumination. Only its full mastery will enable the photographer to visualise freely and individualistically instead of forcing him on to the easier but tedious path of imitative thinking.

THE DIRECTION OF LIGHT

The direction of light determines the form of an object. The term "direction of light" describes *the relation of the light-incidence to the line of camera-vision. The smaller the angle between these two lines—i.e. the more they coincide—the flatter appears the image. The more the angle between these two lines widens towards 90°, the more contrast is created.* As the angle widens towards 180°, the shadow element becomes more predominant until the area of light is ultimately confined to a very narrow rim.

It is difficult to give rules, but we can safely say that the best form-rendering of a three-dimensional object is achieved by a light which meets the line of camera-vision at an angle between 45° and 90°. The exact position at which a lamp should be placed in order to give the ideal form rendering cannot be theoretically determined, as it varies according to the form of the object.

The need for intelligent planning becomes all the more stressed by the fact that the direction of light is also instrumental in forming the character of the picture.

We shall see later how the existence of shadow helps to create a dramatic effect and that the dramatic impression becomes more emphasised as the shadow element of the picture becomes more pronounced. In other words: *the larger the angle between the line of light-incidence and the line of camera-vision, the more "dramatic" is the pictorial effect.*

One would assume that every photographer, appreciating the great importance of the direction of light, preconsiders the placing of his lamps most carefully. Unfortunately there are only too many who prefer a "safe" lighting (*i.e.* a flat, shallow and senseless flooding of the object which avoids "dangerous" shadows) to the more strenuous occupation of logical thinking and experiment. I advise the student most strongly to spare no effort to learn how an object (it may be a face, a flower-bowl or a match-box) alters its appearance under the varying angles of light incidence. These experiments are very easily executed. All one needs is a single lamp which is to be moved slowly around the object, and the patience necessary to study and note the varying changes effected in this way. (See pp. 78/79.)

TERMS

The photographer has terms which he needs for describing certain kinds of lighting. These terms are based on the position of the light source in its relation to the object. (See p. 77.)

We start with *front-lighting* or *central lighting*, i.e. a light produced by a light source placed right in front of the object. If we now move the light source *horizontally* we obtain *side-lighting*, and when continuing this movement *rim-lighting* and, finally, *back-lighting*.

If we move the light source *vertically* (again starting from a front position) we will obtain *top-lighting* or *under-lighting* respectively and when carried far enough again rim- or back-lighting.

Moving the lamp *diagonally upwards*, we obtain *cross-lighting* which is, as we shall see later, most useful in portraiture and figure photography.

THE FIRST STEP: VISUALISING

Before you move a single lamp—indeed, before you even decide what lighting to employ for the making of a picture—make up your mind what you want to do. Visualise composition and pictorial balance after knowing what you wish your picture to express.

Before deciding on the particular lighting technique to be employed for your pictorial problem, you must *feel* the "atmosphere" you want to convey. A rough rule to remember is, that *pictures full of shadow or darkness* (low-key pictures) *have a greater tendency to create emotional effects than those lighting compositions which consist predominantly of light and subtle middle tones* (high-key pictures).

Only after having planned the atmosphere you want to create within your picture, can you select the kind of lighting and, consequently, the kind of lamps you are going to use. If we look back we shall find that the different kinds of light sources and the special diffusers used in combination with various negative materials give us a complete control.

Allowing for exceptions to the rule, we can safely assume that *soft effects find their applications mostly in "high-key" pictures, while "low-*

76

DIFFERENT SPECTRA COMPARED: *Left:* Water colour palette lit by 3,200°K flood. *Right:* Water colour palette by fluorescent room lighting in blacked-out room.

DIRECT AND INDIRECT LIGHTING COMBINED: *Left:* Glass with 3,200°K spot lighting on white background with slight direct light spill on to the glass. *Right:* Same lighting scheme but with added reflection into glass from red paper reflector.

 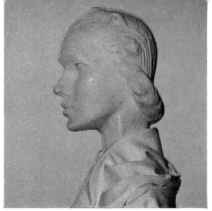 

LIGHT AND COLOUR: *Above left:* Silhouette with 3,200°K flood. Light on blue paper background only ($\frac{1}{2}$ sec. at *f*16). *Above right:* Semi-silhouette; as previous picture but with added fill-in light off-centre, level on near side.

Column on right. *Top:* Main light off-centre on far side. 3,200°K spot plus background lighting by two floods 3,200°K ($\frac{1}{2}$ sec. at *f*16). *Upper centre:* As above but with added fill-in flood at 3,200°K ($\frac{1}{2}$ sec. at *f*22). *Lower centre:* As above but fill-in flood is half the distance from the model ($\frac{1}{2}$ sec. at *f*22). *Bottom:* As above but exposure halved ($\frac{1}{4}$ sec. at *f*22) thus creating higher contrast. Compare this result with upper centre.

78

Column on right. *Top:* Frontal lighting by 3,200°K spot. Rear lighting by photoflood at 3,450°K ($\frac{1}{4}$ sec. at f22). Note warmer "white" on front against colder "white" on back of head. *Upper centre:* Use of reflected light from red paper. Two floods at 3,200°K on background. *Lower centre:* Main light at 3,200°K with indirect fill-in lighting from red paper. *Bottom:* Main light by 3,200°K spot through magenta light filter. Fill-in light by 3,200°K flood unfiltered.

Below: As last three examples on opposite page, but fill-in light now by domestic bulb at 2,750°K. Note yellow cast in shadow.

BUILDING UP COLOUR: *Top:* Fabric lit only by main light at 3,200°K. *Upper centre:* Main light at 3,200°K plus indirect lighting from red paper. *Lower centre:* Main light at 3,200°K plus direct lighting from spot through red light filter. *Bottom:* Main light at 3,200°K plus two added lights. One spot with red and another spot with yellow light filter.

key" treatment depends more on hard contrasts and "*bite*". Generally, subjects with a masculine flair require a bold and vigorous approach, while pictures featuring the feminine element usually "cry" for softness, half-tones and glamour.

THE SECOND STEP: THE BASIC LIGHT

Every lighting scheme must be built up *logically*. Artificial lighting as employed for photography should not be the outcome of a haphazard playing about, for we can only build up lighting according to our intentions if we develop it by a systematic method of working progressively step by step. It will not do to switch on all the lamps at once, shifting them here and there and hoping for the best.

Make it a habit to shut out all daylight or unwanted artificial light before starting with the building up of the lighting. When working with artificial lighting it is essential that you have every effect and all the tone-values of your composition strictly under control; this is, however, only possible if any incidental stray lighting is eliminated.

Start your lighting with one lamp only: the basic light. This light is not called "basic" merely because it constitutes the first practical step, but because it is the light which must in itself demonstrate the intentions of the photographer in a rough manner; it must therefore also govern all subsequent lighting developments.

It has to be realised that the term "basic light" does not refer to any special kind of light. Here are a few examples.

If we wish to treat the subject as a silhouette or half-silhouette, the basic light will obviously be a light illuminating the background. In a pure silhouette (p. 116) this basic light will constitute the total amount of lighting needed in the picture.

In the semi-silhouette (p. 121) the basic light is again the lighting on the background, but it is supplemented by a more or less diffused light on the subject. The supplementary light serves to lighten the subject and to bring it into the right relationship with the luminosity of the background.

On the other hand, if we wish to photograph a profile portrait and emphasise the facial characteristics by a vigorous rim of light (p. 121) along its contours, the basic light will be the rim light. The tone of the background and the further light effects on the face will have to be regarded as of secondary importance.

THE THIRD STEP: THE SUPPLEMENTARY LIGHT

While the basic light is mostly produced by one lamp only, the secondary or supplementary light can be created by any number of

81

lamps. The purpose of every supplementary light is to bring the idea roughly indicated by the basic light to pictorial completeness. *In no circumstances should the supplementary light contradict the meaning of the basic light*, but always emphasise its significance.

If we again take the example of a face in profile which is basically lit by a rim of light along its outline, the supplementary lights employed in such a picture would be:

First Supplementary Light: on background if we wish to have a background other than black.

Second Supplementary Light: a general flood on the face to bring the completely black parts of the face up to a standard of luminosity which conforms with our intention.

Third Supplementary Light: Spot-light effect from behind the sitter so as to produce a new rim light along the back of the sitter's head, at the same time lighting up the hair.

I want to mention at this stage that *if the object is detached from the background, object (foreground unit) and background should be lighted as separate units*, even when they form one entity in composition. Only thus is it possible to control the tone values on the background.

BACKGROUND PROJECTION

Until recently background projection was produced by a type of spot-light projector fitted with a projector lamp. This method had many shortcomings and it was most difficult to obtain realistic effects.

The latest optical method of front projection upon a special "glass" screen has proved very much more effective.

This technique can now be used, often very convincingly, to give naturalistic backgrounds in monochrome and colour for certain types of fashion or advertising illustration when it is not feasible to produce the real thing on location which, of course, is always preferable.

This technique requires very expensive equipment and is only for the professional photographer.

DAYLIGHT

It is nowadays only seldom that a professional studio photographer mixes daylight and artificial light. To him this combination does not offer any advantages which would compensate for the loss of reliability incurred by the ever-changing conditions of daylight.

For the amateur, however, this combination is still of great importance. Most amateurs have only a limited number of lamps at their disposal, and they seldom possess a spot-light by which they can obtain the brilliant highlights and well-defined shadow forms of direct sunlight.

The method to be employed in building up the lighting is here exactly the same as when working with artificial lighting. Again we have to start with one light source only—namely, with the one creating the *basic* light. When employing direct sunlight we shall use this as the basic light source and treat it like a spot-light. We shall then use our (weaker) artificial-light sources—or reflector—for the secondary effects, such as shadow dilution or supplementary highlights.

If we have only diffused daylight at our disposal, we shall produce our basic light with the artificial-light source and use the daylight as "flood".

I do not recommend the use of combined artificial lighting and daylight for *still-life* photography because of the inflexibility of the daylight source. Especially when dealing with small objects this short-coming becomes clearly apparent. For portrait studies, on the other hand, this kind of light combination can be employed to great advantage, and one must not limit one's experiments to purely "straight shots". Even big close-ups and angle shots can be most effectively handled in this way. Here, as everywhere else, the result depends to a far greater extent on the talent and skill of the photographer than on his equipment. Indeed, one photo-flood bulb in a reflector, one sheet of white paper and a window is an absolutely sufficient and excellent equipment for a wide range of photographic possibilities.

Professionally this technique of combining daylight and artificial lighting is used extensively by press and illustrative photographers who often use one or more flash-heads in conjunction with sunlight or an overcast sky. (See p. 71.)

Similarly the industrial photographer often uses artificial lighting (spot-lights, Colortran, flash) under daylight conditions, when the daylight coming from the large overhead skylights establishes a high level of general illumination. Under these circumstances it is often essential to use artificial light sources of great power to count era all-over flatness and to emphasise detail.

PRIMITIVE LIGHT SOURCES

Primitive light sources, such as a match, candle or oil lamp, etc., are not to be assessed as tools for creating a photographic image, but merely as "props" serving to enhance the pictorial effect or to tell a story.

This statement does not imply that there are no circumstances when a primitive light source can be used successfully in the making of a photograph; but the occasions when a candle or a camp fire constitutes the only source of photographic lighting are rare. The primitive

83

light source does not freely adapt itself to the intentions of the photographer; anyway, it would be futile to use light sources of inadequate intensity when even the amateur has cheap and efficient photographic lamps at his disposal.

Another point not to be overlooked is that although a situation might appear to our eye as picturesque in the romantic light of a coal fire or the halo of an oil lamp, it does not necessarily follow that it will be registered just as attractively by the camera; in fact, we shall often find when examining our negative that contrasts have been exaggerated and a great amount of "atmosphere" lost.

However, do not let us condemn the primitive light source as being unable to help the photographer. Quite the contrary; the primitive light source properly handled can greatly contribute to pictorial expression and to a lifelike representation of certain settings. We all know, for instance, the pictures which show a man lighting his cigarette or the candle on the Christmas tree—indeed, there is hardly a photographer who has not tried his hand on those or similar subjects at one time or another. The candle, especially, offers many pictorial opportunities. Although the eye does not register a halo around the flame, we are now accustomed—undoubtedly through the influence of innumerable paintings—to associate a burning candle with this halo and to consider it an essential—indeed intrinsic—asset to its atmosphere. *The photographer who wishes to produce this glamorous halo effect should use an unbacked plate.* Films and backed negative materials are unsuitable for this purpose.

A candle has also the advantage over similar light sources that it burns off with a comparatively steady flame, and thus facilities long exposure times. Still, even a long exposure time does not help us to overcome the *excessive* contrast always produced by a primitive light source because of its smallness and the absence of reflected light. It is consequently necessary to give at least one supplementary light which renders detail which otherwise would be lost.

In other words: to make the best of these assets the photographer must look at the primitive light source as just another object in the picture while he produces his main lighting with a proper *photographic* light source.

A picture in which a primitive light source is included needs special lighting treatment and here are a few hints on the subject:

(1) The lighting should be simple.

(2) The lighting should not contradict the pictorial situation.

(3) A primitive light source should only be included in a picture when the pictorial plot warrants it.

(4) When including a primitive light source in a picture one must also show the reason for its existence and the atmosphere surrounding it.

84

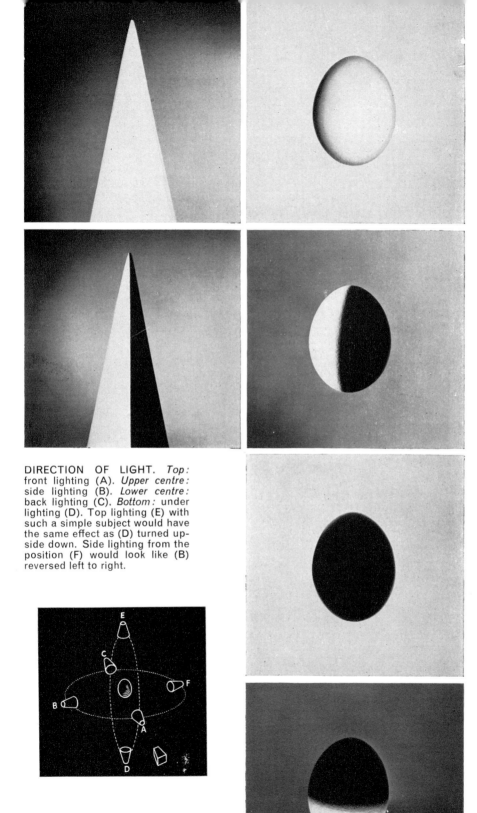

DIRECTION OF LIGHT. *Top:* front lighting (A). *Upper centre:* side lighting (B). *Lower centre:* back lighting (C). *Bottom:* under lighting (D). Top lighting (E) with such a simple subject would have the same effect as (D) turned up-side down. Side lighting from the position (F) would look like (B) reversed left to right.

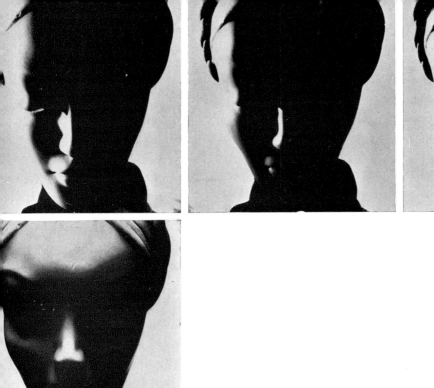

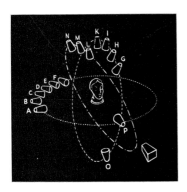

DIRECTION OF LIGHT. *Upper row :* the effect of moving the light from the position of acute side light (A) to almost back light (F). *Upper centre row :* the effect of moving the light upwards from the position (G) to (K), the latter being acute top lighting. *Lower centre row :* the effect of moving the light diagonally from the position (L) to (N). *Bottom left :* under lighting (O). *Bottom right :* dead front lighting (P).

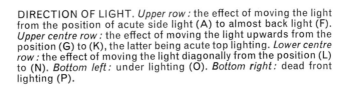

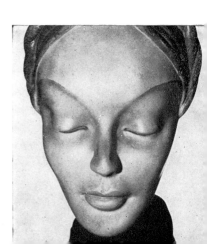

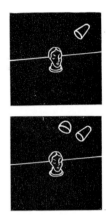

BUILDING UP THE LIGHTING.
Top: spot light serves as basic light. *Upper centre:* a flood has been added as a supplementary to produce rim highlight on left cheek. *Lower centre:* a bank of floods has been introduced in front of the subject to give general illumination. *Bottom:* special lighting for the background brings relief and the finishing touch.

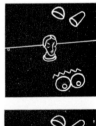

SHADOW DEFINITION. *Top:* spot light producing sharply defined shadows. *Upper centre:* flood leading to a softer type of light. *Lower centre:* diffused flood and diffused shadow. *Bottom:* double lighting means doubling the shadow. If symmetrically arranged, as in this case, a pleasing shadow pattern may be produced.

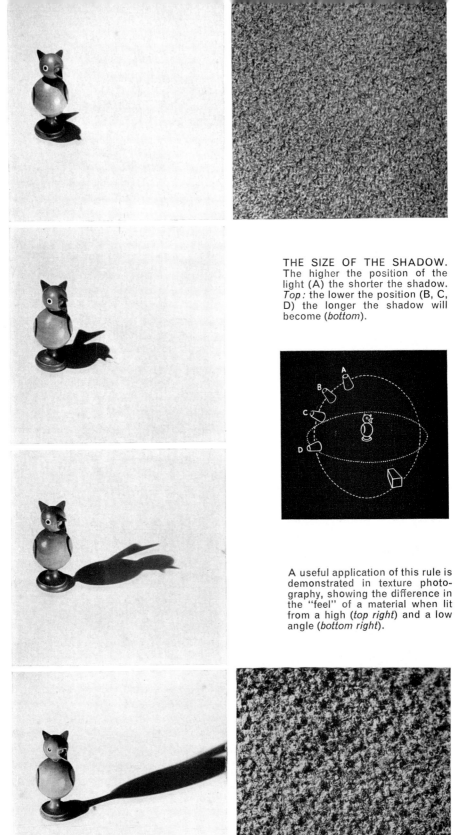

THE SIZE OF THE SHADOW.
The higher the position of the light (A) the shorter the shadow. *Top:* the lower the position (B, C, D) the longer the shadow will become (*bottom*).

A useful application of this rule is demonstrated in texture photography, showing the difference in the "feel" of a material when lit from a high (*top right*) and a low angle (*bottom right*).

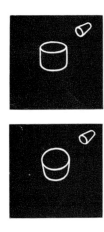

THE SHAPE OF THE SHADOW is essentially influenced by the position of the subject. Even a subject of a comparatively simple outline may produce intricate shadow patterns with its position in relation to the background carefully chosen. Note that the position of the light source has been left unchanged in all the four pictures.

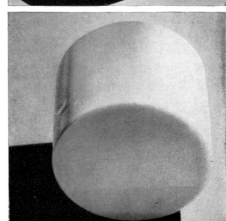

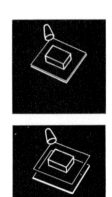

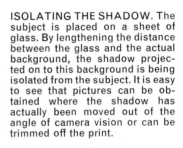

ISOLATING THE SHADOW. The subject is placed on a sheet of glass. By lengthening the distance between the glass and the actual background, the shadow projected on to this background is being isolated from the subject. It is easy to see that pictures can be obtained where the shadow has actually been moved out of the angle of camera vision or can be trimmed off the print.

THE SHADOW

Light and shade are for the photographer more than facts of physics, more than questions of technical construction. Light and shade are not merely extraneous agents making things perceptible to vision or helping to create images on negatives, but are the intrinsic forces which give photography justification for its existence. One can go even further and say that the "translation" of light and shade into terms of optical *and* sensorial impressions *is* photography.

It is obvious that this task of photography can only be performed if the photographer is able to control light and shadow, and to apply their possibilities according to his wish. It is also essential that the photographer know by practical experience the many and varied groupings of available light sources, so that he can visualise the intended and final result, before he has started to move even a single lamp.

Here the question arises whether it is advisable to evolve a number of "standard schemes" of lighting which can be employed in turn on different occasions. I am of the opinion that such standard schemes can do more harm than good, for they so often tend to lead to mental inflexibility and to a general mechanisation of technique. Please bear in mind that when in later pages I give certain "light schemes" and examples, these are intended to serve merely as a general guide and not as a ready-made solution for all photographic problems.

TYPES OF SHADOWS

We must first understand what we mean by the term "shadow". We shall distinguish between the *true shadow* and the *bogus shadow*.

The true shadow—or the cast shadow, to call it by its more common name—is an area from which light is partially or totally eliminated by a more or less opaque obstacle introduced between the light source and the base of projection. Needless to say, the obstacle has to be smaller than the beam of light. Characteristic of the true (cast) shadow is its *dependence on the existence of a light-obstructing substance*. It will therefore have a definite shape—a shape primarily depending on the form of the subject.

The bogus shadow is an area from which light is partially or totally eliminated. Characteristic of the bogus shadow is that it does not depend on a substance, but that it is *merely a matter of tone-gradation* produced by a deterioration of light.

From the psychological point of view, the bogus shadow can have the same effect as the true shadow. *Both* types of shadow are able to evoke thought-associations and create what we call "atmosphere". Considered from the viewpoint of lighting technique, however, it is imperative that we adhere to the differentiation between the cast true shadow and the bogus shadow. It must be realised that we can control a cast shadow to a far greater extent than a bogus shadow. While the tone, definition, shape and size of a true shadow can be widely influenced by varying methods, the bogus shadow depends to such a degree on the surface-form of the object or on the character of our light source that its construction is more or less incidental.

The next sections make the greater adaptability of the cast shadow clearly apparent and demonstrate the different methods of shadow control. But we shall also revert to the bogus shadow, which has its own problems and its individual pictorial significance.

THE TONE OF THE CAST SHADOW

We have to distinguish between a "pure" and a "diluted" shadow. By pure shadow we mean that the shadow is completely black, by diluted shadow it is lightened up to varying degrees. *The smaller the light source and the nearer the shadow-casting object is to the background the "purer" will be the shadow.*

Just hold your outstretched hand between an ordinary lamp and a light surface, e.g. a light table-top. Naturally you will obtain a shadow. Now you will note that when you hold your hand *very* close to the table, the shadow is practically pure, but when you move your hand slightly higher, away from the table, you will obtain a lighter edge around a pure-black shadow nucleus. The pure, inner part is called the *Umbra*, the lighter, outer part the *Penumbra*. Now you will observe that the farther you remove your hand from the table, the larger will become the penumbra and the smaller the umbra, until the hand is so far away that the shadow is totally penumbral. This means that the pure, umbral nucleus has been lost and that all which remains is a shadow which is grey or diluted.

94

If you now repeat this experiment with a small light source you will see that you can remove your hand much farther away from the table than before and still retain a comparatively pure shadow.

These facts become important when you project a shadow on to a background which is detached from the shadow-casting object. On the other hand, it is plain that they lose a lot of their usefulness for tone-control when the object is connected with the background, as, in this case, the distance between object and projection-base is always comparatively small and the shadow therefore more or less pure.

If we wish to control the tone of a shadow under the latter conditions we must use another method (*i.e. employ a supplementary light*). This second method is the practical one, because it can be more universally employed. It can be used equally well whether the shadow is annexed (*i.e.* linked up with the shadow-casting substance) or when it is isolated (*i.e.* detached from the object).

One just has to take a second lamp and lighten the shadow to the desired degree. There are, however, a few points which have to be watched.

First of all, it must be remembered that the second light has in this case the sole purpose of lighting an existing shadow—not producing a new one. It will therefore be necessary either to direct the light from such an angle that no new shadow is produced, or, since this is not always possible, one must use a light source which, by its nature, will not produce a shadow too easily, or in any case only a very faint one. The safest light source is here not a lamp, but a sheet of mat white board which lightens the shadows by reflection only.

In colour photography, we have to consider not only the density at the shadow but also its hue. This depends on the colour of the reflector screen or the colour of the object casting the shadow, or both.

In order to avoid misunderstandings I wish to say that there are, of course, occasions when two shadows from one single object are desired—for instance, in order to make a shadow pattern. In that part in which two diluted shadows overlap, the shadow will become more or less pure. This has, however, nothing to do with tone-control, but with composition.

Some may now ask how dark or how light a shadow should be. There is one rule which can be considered valid for most occasions: *the purer the shadow the more predominant, the more diluted the more insignificant will it appear in the picture*. Some people believe that there should be "drawing in the shadow"—that it should be kept light enough to make the structure of the underlying surface still discernible. Good advice as that may be in many cases, it is definitely not good enough to be acclaimed as a rule. The thesis would, first of all, only be applicable to "body-shadows", and not to fine "line-shadows". Secondly, it leaves out of account the many expressive possibilities of a heavy silhouette treatment. I am the last person to advocate anything like uncontrolled and meaningless black patches which seem to have no other task in a picture but to disturb the pictorial composition, and consequently to irritate the spectator. At the same time, however, I would suggest that in many cases it is often just the pure shadow, with its extinction of underlying detail, which can evoke in us the sensation of darkness with all its pictorial significance.

DEFINITION OF THE CAST SHADOW

The term shadow-definition refers to either the "hardness" or "softness" of a shadow, meaning whether its *edges* are sharp or fuzzy. Definition depends on the same factors as the tone of a shadow (see p. 94): firstly, on the *size and construction of the light source, and* secondly on the *distance of the obstructive substance from the projection-base.*

This implies that, having these two factors under one's control, the definition of a shadow can be produced according to one's own free will and intention; it is not the accidental outcome of existing lighting conditions which cannot be modified. It now becomes apparent how important it is to take the greatest care in choosing the right type of lamp for the job.

It has already been mentioned that the smaller the light source the better defined is the shadow. We have also seen that the carbon-arc spot-light is for this reason the most suitable light source to employ when a clear-cut shadow is required. A soft shadow can be produced by employing a lamp with a comparatively extensive filament design fixed in a broad and shallow reflector.

The second factor influencing shadow-definition is the distance between the object casting the shadow and the projection-base. The nearer the object is to the projection-base the sharper will be the edges of the shadow, and *vice versa*.

Choose an object which promises to give a simple but impressive shadow pattern (*e.g.* a piece of wire netting), and move it slowly to and fro between light source and projection-base. Observe well and make notes on lighting employed, distances, etc., and then repeat the experiment with other light sources. You will find the comparison of your notes both absorbing and interesting, all the more so as the quality of the shadow is not only important for composition but also accentuates to a certain degree the character of the subject by which it is cast.

For instance, visualise a pair of scissors. We are accustomed to

96

associate them with sharpness—the keenness of the blades. It is obvious that, if we wish to include the shadow of the scissors in the picture, we must present it as being well defined, with the sharp edge intrinsic to the subject. Wilful diffusion on the shadow in this case would result in an effect which would deprive the subject of one of its characteristic attributes.

SHAPE AND SIZE OF A CAST SHADOW

While the definition of a shadow depends on the kind of light source and on the distance of the obstructive substance from the projection surface, the shape and size of a shadow depend on the following three factors: (1) *distance of object to base of projection*. (2) *Relative position of light source (angle of light-incidence) and angle of object to projection-base*. (3) *Surface-form of projection-base*, i.e. *if the base is plain, convex or concave*. Let us take these points one by one.

(1) The first thing to be realised is that the distance between object and projection-base and the distance between lamp and object can only influence the *size* of the shadow—not its shape. This means that there are three ways of altering the size of a shadow: first to introduce a larger object of exactly the same shape into the same position as the original shadow-casting obstacle—leaving the projection-base unmoved; secondly to move the light source farther away from the subject without altering the angle of light-incidence and the position of the object; thirdly to move the projection-base farther away from the object. *The greater the distance between object and projection-base the larger will be the shadow*. It is obvious that the smallest possible size of a shadow is the size of the object which produces it.

(2) The relative positions of object and projection-base, as well as the angle of light-incidence, influence the shape *and* size of the shadow simultaneously. One can alter size *and* shape of a shadow in two ways: either by *altering the position of the object in relation to the background, without moving the light source—or by altering the angle of light-incidence without altering the position of object or background*.

The first method must necessarily be employed when it is impossible to move the light source. This method also produces a greater number of different shadow-forms. The second method has, however, the advantage that it facilitates more subtle changes and slight differentiations than does the first, which tends to alter the shape of the shadow rather too drastically.

There is the classical rule that *if the light falls at an angle of 45° the length of a shadow is equal to the height of the object. The larger the angle, the shorter becomes the shadow*, and *vice versa*. This means that the longest shadow is produced by a light-incidence of approximately

1°, the shortest shadow by lighting directly from the top, *i.e.* from an angle of 90°.

(3) The third factor determining the size and shape of a shadow is the surface-form of the background on to which the shadow is projected (*i.e.* whether it is plain, concave or convex). The influence which the surface-form of the projection-base (or background) has on the shape of a shadow is negligible, but the size (especially the length) of a shadow can be altered by it quite drastically. The method of altering the surface-form of the background is chiefly of theoretical interest—occasions for its successful practical application are somewhat rare.

It will therefore suffice to know that: *A concave projection-base always shortens a shadow. A convex projection-base may either shorten or lengthen the shadow, this being dependent on the grade and kind of bend. The shape of the shadow adjusts itself to the bend of the projection-base.*

DOMINANCE OF CAST SHADOWS

Here again it must be realised that "form of shadow" is not merely a consequence of physical laws having a bearing on aesthetic considerations, such as pictorial composition. No; the form of a shadow is an essential means of enabling the photographer to express a certain message in his picture and to get it over to the spectator. The practical importance of the implications of this point must not be underrated.

For instance, allowing for the exception to the rule, it is obvious that the larger the shadow the more important is the role it plays in the picture. It is also plain that, the larger the shadow in comparison with the object which casts it, the more will it dominate the object. This statement is not quite so straightforward as it may seem at a first glance, for the dominance of a shadow can be of two kinds—concrete or abstract. The first is perceptible by vision, the second only by imagination.

Concrete dominance is created by the fact that the space covered by the shadow is comparatively extensive; in consequence the spectator will acknowledge the shadow as a unit of special pictorial importance. This applies specially to texture-photography, which is nothing but the wilful exaggeration of the shadow element by means of an acute and well-defined angle-lighting. The rendering of photographic texture is achieved by elongating the individual shadow particles cast by the surface texture of the object to such an extent that their size is out of proportion to the one created and perceived under ordinary lighting conditions.

Abstract dominance rests in the "dramatic" quality of the shadow. Everyone can visualise, for instance, how a silhouette lifts the pictorial

98

subject out of humdrum reality into the region of the unreal, how the shadow of a man in a raincoat cast on to a brick wall can convert a quite ordinary pictorial situation into a murder story, and how the gruesome effect can still be magnified by elongating the shadow.

THE BOGUS SHADOW

We have seen (p. 93) that, while the cast (true) shadow depends on a light-obstructing substance, the bogus shadow is nothing but an absence of light caused by a bend in an object's surface or by the limited range of illumination from the artificial-light source.

To illustrate the first type of bogus shadow we merely have to visualise a face on which there is a typical play of light and shade. The shadow cast by the nose is obviously a true shadow. But the shadow on the cheek is a bogus shadow—a mere absence of light. Similarly any unilluminated part of a sphere (or rounded object) is a bogus shadow, while the shaded area cast by that sphere (or object) upon its background is a true shadow.

The bogus shadow is instrumental in rendering form. *The softer its edge the softer and rounder will the object appear ; the harder its edge the more angular the result.* The degree of hardness of the shadow edge is determined first by the form of the object itself, and secondly by the quality of the light. For instance: the roundness of a face lends itself better to angular shadow-forms than the roundness of a sphere, and the soft light of a flood produces softer forms than the hard light propagated by a spot-light lamp.

The second type of bogus shadow can best be illustrated by projecting a spot of light upon a flat surface. We shall then see that *the area outside the field of illumination* appears to be dark—"in shadow". Here the difference between the cast shadow and the bogus shadow becomes obvious. The definition of the bogus shadow can be controlled by the choice of the illuminating lamp; needless to repeat that a spot-light gives a harder light than a flood and that, when using a flood, the distance between light source and projection-base has a strong bearing on the effect.

The shape of this second type of bogus shadow depends entirely on the angle at which the light meets the projection-base. When the lamp shines upon it from in front, the shadow-area will encompass a round area of light, while a spot-light placed near the background and shining upon it at a very oblique angle produces two shadow areas distinctly separated by a beam of light, the edges of which run more or less parallel.

In practice we shall soon learn how the bogus shadow presents itself in the picture sometimes merely as a small, incidental unit and sometimes as the planned dynamic base of the picture.

99

THE ANNEXED CAST SHADOW

A shadow is "annexed" when it is *cast by an object which is linked up with the projection-base, i.e.* if the shadow-producing substance stands or leans directly on its background or is naturally attached to it.

Examples of an annexed shadow are, for instance, the shadow of the nose or the texture-shadows in a piece of fabric. It is obvious that these types of shadow—resulting from the moulding of the subject's surface—can never be converted into isolated shadow-forms. There are other kinds of annexed shadows—for example, those produced by a vase standing on a table or a figure leaning against a pillar—which can be made into isolated shadows easily enough. One has just to lift the vase up from the table or place the figure a little distance away from the background.

It is typical of the annexed shadow that the spectator takes its existence for granted. The spectator hardly notes its presence in a picture as long as the shadow is not strengthened and individualised to such an extent that he recognises it as something out of the ordinary, something he is not accustomed to seeing in everyday life.

The reason for this is obvious: everyone knows that whenever an object is lighted it must provide a shadow somewhere—unless the light-beam is too small to envelop the object. Our memory is not impressed by those few instances where the shadow evades our mechanical vision on account of some abnormal diffusion of the light source, purely reflective backgrounds or other similar influences.

It follows that the photographer has to accentuate strongly the form of the annexed shadow if he wishes to lift it out of its Cinderella existence. But here a warning might not be misplaced. The flexibility of technique which enables us to "mould" shadow and raise it from relative insignificance to a highly expressive and creative agent must not be absued in an irresponsible manner. The artificial bolstering up of the shadow must not be misused for the sake of cheap effects, nor for purely "formal" reasons. This is done much too often. Indeed, photography today tends to give too much importance to purely ornamental shadow-forms, and to dwell in an exuberance of pattern for its own sake.

This habit of presenting shadow as an aesthetic superficiality must lead to a point when the spectator will recognise it merely as a shallow, commonplace fabrication. Photography will thus lose one of the few means by which it can hope to emancipate itself from its mechanical, solely representational status.

Especially regarding still-life photography I advise the student to take the annexed shadow for just what it really is—the companion to the main object illustrated. He should realise that the shadow should help to make the best of the object, not think that the only excuse for

100

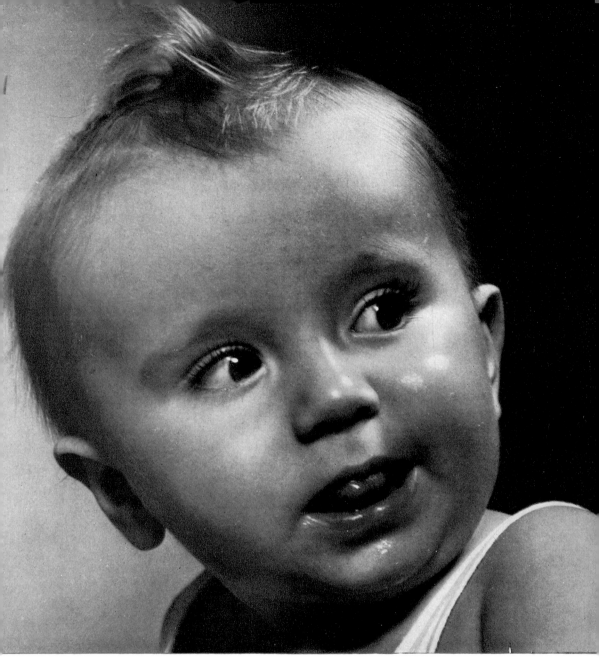

LIGHTING AS A MEANS TO NATURAL MODELLING. Artificial lighting is employed here in its most unobtrusive manner. It does not appear as such at all, but just helps to depict the head in its natural roundness. Phot: *Torkel Korling, Chicago.*

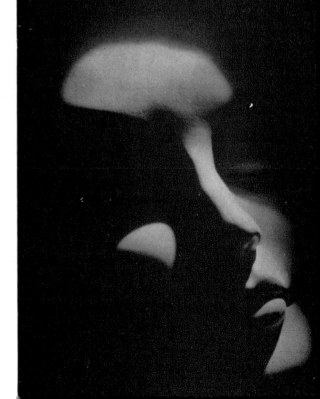

102

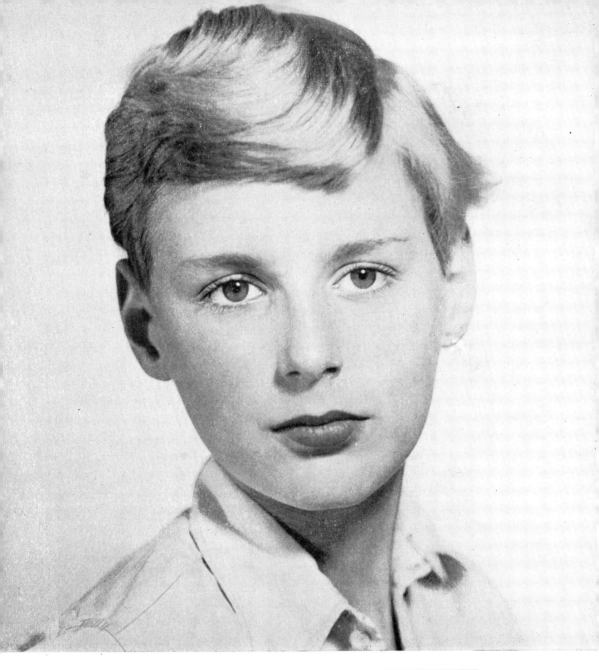

PICTORIALLY CREATIVE LIGHTING. *On page* 102. The choice of the lamp and its positioning enable the photographer to bring to almost every face a story of its own. Phot: *W. Nurnberg, London.*

HIGH-KEY PORTRAIT. The basic lighting is that on the background which establishes the tone to which the flesh tones have to be approximated. In this picture a strong modelling light was used on the head, but the resulting shadows subsequently lighted up by a secondary flood. Phot: *A. J. Coppel, London.*

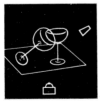

LIGHTING WITHOUT BACKGROUND SHADOW. The use of a glass base and a removed background leads to isolation of the shadow and leaves the subject apparently suspended in an undefined space. This is a successful method of lighting for still life and commercial work. Phot: *Alexander, London.*

the object's presence in the picture is its faculty of producing an "interesting shadow". After all, it is the purpose of all pictures either to portray objects, animate or inanimate, or to express the photographer's attitude to them—form and composition being subordinated to these ends.

THE ISOLATED SHADOW

A shadow is "isolated" when it is *projected by an object which is separated from its background, i.e.* when the shadow-casting substance is placed some distance away from the projection-base.

The "isolated" shadow presents to the photographer technical possibilities which an annexed shadow is unable to give. Here are a few examples:

Although an isolated shadow may be optically perceived as if it is "grown on" to the subject, it is in fact a distance away from it. This *enables the photographer to give additional lighting to the subject without touching the shadow,* and therefore without altering its tone-value. In particular, symmetrical outline effects can be produced by means of highlights around the subject, without the loss of any purity and definition in the shadow; were the shadow annexed to the subject this would not be possible because the lights which create these highlight effects must then also touch the background to which the object is attached, and thus either produce a new shadow pattern or lighten the main shadow-unit, or both.

The detachment of the object from its background also makes it *possible to alter the tone-value of the background* without at the same time altering the tone-value of the object. This is, however, not all. The isolation of the shadow from its substance offers still further advantages.

We have seen (p. 97) that the only method of altering the size of a shadow without simultaneously altering its shape or the size of the shadow-casting object, is to move the object farther away from the projection-base. From this it follows that the isolated shadow treatment not only enables us *to alter the size of the shadow itself according to our wish,* but also to alter the relation between object and shadow in respect of size and pictorial (or psychological) importance.

THE SILHOUETTE SHADOW

The isolated shadow presents itself in its purest form in the "silhouette". Here the pictorial detachment from the object is complete and the shadow takes on a life of its own; it is the shadow—not the object itself—which tells the story in the picture.

The silhouette tends to evoke a certain feeling of unreality. This statement should not be misinterpreted. One is too easily tempted to associate with the term unreality a mystical gloom or a sinister, fathomless symbolism. It should, however, be realised that this constitutes only one side of the Unreal. Gay and joyful exhilaration can also be lifted into the spheres of unreality without its light-heartedness being lost in the process.

Silhouettes can be cast either by any object which lends itself to this purpose, or by a flat (cardboard) mask which represents certain settings, such as a window with flower-pots, a motor-car, a ship, etc. Besides these naturalistic subjects one can choose to cut masks which represent merely some kind of geometrical pattern.

A pure and well-defined image is usually expected of a silhouette and it is for this reason that a *spot-light or a similar light source should be employed* for its production. For the benefit of the professional photographer special projectors have been marketed into which masks can be inserted between the projector lamp and a lens.

A further point to be particularly remembered is that *the lighting of the foreground unit must never touch the background* on to which the silhouette has been cast. Stray lighting will weaken the silhouette image considerably, sometimes nearly to extinction, or the shadows of the foreground unit may interfere with the silhouette. It is therefore advisable to employ spot-lights and *not* flood-lamps for the lighting of the foreground unit.

Silhouette-shadows can also be produced in an entirely different way, by projecting the shadow image from behind a translucent background. When employing this method we have to remember, firstly, that the object is to be placed very near to the background and, secondly, that the light source be a good distance away from the object but, at the same time, completely hidden by it. Only then can we achieve a clear-cut shadow image and also a background which is *evenly* lit. The method of projecting a shadow in this way has two advantages. It produces an image free of distortion and is also more convenient for the amateur. He who may either be restricted in working space or has no suitable wall space can overcome his difficulties by taking a large linen sheet which he fastens into a door frame and by placing object and light source in one room and his camera in the other.

Needless to state there must be no other kind of illumination in either room while the photograph is being taken.

Background silhouettes must not be confused with what is commonly called "background-projection". This term does not refer to shadow-projection at all, but to a technique by which lantern slides are projected on to a screen. The fundamental difference between those two kinds of projection technique lies in the fact that "background-projection" (see p. 82) aims at a realistic, three-dimensional effect, while the silhouette can never create more than a plain, *two*-dimensional impression.

OTHER KINDS OF ISOLATED CAST SHADOW

We have seen that the silhouette is the prototype of the isolated shadow because it is isolated from the object to such an extent that the object is entirely excluded from the picture. Not every isolated shadow is, however, detached to this extent. It can stand—pictorially— "beside" the object, or even be partially overlapped by it, so that it vanishes, more or less, behind the shadow-producing substance.

Now, it might be argued that such a shadow which seems to be connected with its subject should not be called "isolated", as it has the same effect on the spectator as any ordinary "annexed" shadow. It must, however, be realised that even if a differentiation may not seem necessary from the viewpoint of final effect, it is essential with regard to the production of a photograph.

SHADOW-FREE TREATMENTS

Shadow-free photography describes two entirely different lighting treatments. The *first* method aims at an *avoidance of cast (true) shadows on the object as well as on its background.* It will be found applied mainly to "high-key" portraiture and nude photography. The *second* method aims at the *complete elimination of cast (true) shadows on the background only,* and is widely used for the normal kind of portrait and figure study and also for special types of still-life photography.

In order to avoid confusion between these two treatments, we shall describe the first as "shadowless photography" and the second as "shadow-free background photography". Both have their individual application, approach and technique. It is therefore essential to investigate the two groups of shadow-free photography separately.

HIGH-KEY PHOTOGRAPHY

A high-key photograph is a picture which is based on a white background and in which light tones are dominating. Any shadows that are existing should be well lit up to a light grey tone. High-key photographs can be produced by means of either tungsten or electronic flash lighting. Direct or bounced lighting can be employed or a combination of both.

The photographer using a high-key technique aims to achieve the following:

(1) To create a two-dimensional, instead of a three-dimensional, effect.

(2) To obtain the greatest possible number of subtle half-tones by sacrificing contrast.

(3) To achieve modelling without the help of dark shadows or without having cast shadows altogether.

High-key pictures created by shadowless photography undoubtedly have their merits. They convey a certain ethereal quality and deftness which no other method is able to achieve. But it is a definitely short-sighted view to see in high-key portrait and figure photography the most desirable form of photography because the wind of changing fashions may favour this subtle imagery from time to time.

High-key lighting is fully justified as an important photographic treatment but not to the exclusion of any other lighting style. No one method should ever be used merely because the photographer happens to consider it "pretty". Whether high-key or chiaroscuro, delicacy of treatment or drama, depends on character or meaning of the subject and the individual photographer's interpretation of it.

There are, as already indicated, different high-key techniques.

To achieve the strictly "classical" high-key photograph, that is to obtain an entire absence of *cast* shadows on subject and background, the general principles are:

(1) The light source to be as near to the lens as is practicable in order to make the line of light incidence coincide with the line of camera-vision. This is most easily achieved by a ring-light unit, a circular flood unit surrounding the camera lens; this can be either a tungsten or electronic flash source. For close-up portraits a soft single flood can also be used but this should then be placed *under* the camera lens and lower than the eye-level of the sitter.

(2) The sitter to be a good distance away from the background.

(3) The white background to be illuminated separately to achieve maximum tone control between foreground and background.

The above "classical" high-key lighting is rarely used nowadays; a modified form of high-key lighting is taking its place which is more easily executed and controlled.

Instead of avoiding cast shadows these are produced in the normal way—often by soft bounced lighting—and then filled in with diffused direct or reflected lighting in the normal way. This method has the advantages that modelling does not rely entirely on the rendering of half-tones. Although negative quality must always be especially good for high-key work, it is not as critical as in true shadowless photography. Hard negative stock should always be avoided and the negatives processed to a low contrast to retain good half-tones and highlights. Excessive over-exposure must be avoided.

SHADOW-FREE BACKGROUND PHOTOGRAPHY

This method means nothing more than the removal of the back-ground-shadow from the picture by isolating the shadow from its substance. There are occasions when the absence of a shadow on the background is an asset. The main purposes to which shadow-free background photography can be applied are threefold: *for "auto-nomous" background treatment; for imitation cut-out aiming at better outline definition of the object;* and *for more successful rendering of certain materials.*

Let us first consider in which way we can best get rid of a shadow from the picture.

If the shadow is annexed this is difficult, although theoretically possible. Indeed, but for one exception, I do not consider the complete elimination of an annexed shadow as a practical (or even desirable) possibility. The one exception mentioned is provided by the *black background*. By taking black silk velvet as background material the shadow is made practically invisible because of the property of the material of absorbing light to such a high degree. No other material than black silk velvet is suitable for a complete suppression of shadow. Black paper or other kinds of black fabric do not lend themselves to this purpose, as they are not sufficiently light-absorbent (see p. 29).

As soon as one wishes to obtain a background which is lighter than "pitch" black, the *only way to eradicate the shadow would be to light it away;* that means to flood the shadow with such an amount of light that it is no longer perceptible to the vision. This method, is however, most unsatisfactory, for the flooding of the shadow will also affect, in most cases, the object, thus making it appear unplastic or texture-less. Now, it might be suggested that the light which is destined to eradicate the shadow could be "spotted" to such an extent and in such a manner that the object and the surrounding background parts are not touched by the light-beam. Theoretically this sounds feasible, but in practice it will be found that it is hardly ever possible to make light behave in such a perfect manner.

For this reason a different method of shadow-elimination had to be found, a method *not* aiming at a "lighting-away" of the shadow. It was found in *excluding the background-shadow from the picture space.* Now, it will be obvious that this can only be made possible if the shadow is completely isolated from its substance and shifted far enough so that it no longer appears inside the picture's frame.

This method presents no special difficulties; if it were possible—as in the production of the silhouette shadow—to separate object and sha-dow to such an extent that the only unit included in the picture was the shadow, it is only logical that using the same means, it should be also possible to retain the object as the sole pictorial unit.

109

Here are two facts which have to be remembered:

The farther the object is placed away from the background the easier it is to produce a shadow-free photograph.

The larger (wider) the angle between the light-beam and the line of camera-vision the easier is it to exclude the shadow from the pictorial frame, the smaller this angle the more difficult will it become. If the line of camera-vision coincides with the line of light, a pictorial separation will be impossible.

When photographing an object *standing in front* of a background, shadow-free background photography is easily accomplished. The process becomes slightly more complicated when photographing an object which must—by its nature—*lie on* a background. In the latter case we may have to *substitute a glass plate for the original background* in order to serve as a base for the object. By fixing the glass plate—which now carries the object—well above the original background we are now able to reproduce an isolated shadow which can be excluded from the picture space in the usual manner. This glass plate should be supported on the corners only. Bulky supports on the side would easily throw additional shadows across the background. The glass plate must be of the finest quality and of course its size adequate to the needs of the picture. If too small a size is chosen, it can easily happen that the edges of the glass plate cast shadows across the camera's field of vision.

The first application of *autonomous background treatment* is that in which the background is to be kept clear not only of shadows cast from the picture's subject, but also from any stray lighting originating from the lights illuminating the subject. By this method one obtains a completely blank background space which can now be treated autonomously, *i.e.* quite for itself without interfering with the lighting on the main subject.

This method is particularly used when "background projection" is to be employed or if one wishes to "paint" the background with light; in portraiture it is most useful because it enables the photographer either to individualise or to generalise the background element and therefore to accentuate or repress it in relation to the foreground unit.

In still-life photography it may become necessary to give different exposure times to foreground and background. The complete separation of foreground and background units achieved by means of shadow-free photography makes it, for instance, possible to expose a dark object in the foreground proportionally longer than its white background, thus avoiding "lack of drawing" in the dark object or an over-exposure of the white background. The value of this technical flexibility is obvious, and the student will find out in his own experiments that this specific aspect of shadow-free photography will

110

help him to overcome problems which otherwise have to be shelved as unsolved.

The second way of application is the *imitation cut-out*. It will be found most useful in connection with still-life photography.

If you look at a catalogue illustrating—let us say—technical instruments, you are bound to run across illustrations which stand well defined in the middle of white space and in which the object is presented without a shadow annexed to it. These effects are usually produced by retouching. Either the background around the object has been covered up with opaque paint on the negative ("blocking out") or colour has been applied around the outlines of the object on the photographic print before being used for blockmaking.

The same result can be achieved by eliminating the background shadow by means of a glass plate (see p. 80). In this way every tone of grey, as well as pure white and black, can easily be produced without necessitating any retouching on the print later on. But this is not the only merit of this method, its main advantage lies in the fact that the object—being placed well away from the background—can be lit from *all* angles, thus facilitating an excellent definition of its outline and a plastic rendering of its form while the background—being undisturbed by shadows—retains its smooth flatness of tone.

The complete removal of background shadows from the picture-space can be of great help to the photographer in his endeavours to reproduce the *shape or the texture* of certain products or materials more faithfully. Especially when tackling transparent matter—glass, transparent plastic—shadow-free background photography is most useful.

The absence of shadow tends to give a certain ethereal quality to a transparent body by removing the feeling of gravity which is always connected with matter, and by putting in its place a feeling of lightness.

But also from a purely photo-technical point of view the shadow-free method has great advantages when photographing transparent objects. Just to give an example, excellent definition of glassware can be achieved by concentrating the lighting solely on the background, as this method eliminates any possible reflection on the surface of the glass object. At the same time there will be no background shadow which could interfere with the sometimes delicate outline and structure of the glass. The latter fact applies especially to cut-glass.

IV THE APPLICATION OF LIGHTING

LIGHT AND SHADOW
AS APPLIED TO FACE AND FIGURE

I have promised not to confront the reader with a set of rigid rules and lighting schemes. The reason for this will now become obvious. When, for instance, watching a human face we find that its form and whole appearance change drastically with every single curve of the head. Sunlight falling upon a face or figure does so without taking the wishes of the photographer into consideration. The photographer has therefore to move his model about until the light shines on it in just the way he wants it to shine. Needless to say that when working with artificial-light sources the shifting is not done to persons, but to lamps.

The term portraiture describes two different kinds of photographic activity: either photographing a person for the sake of achieving a likeness or the subjective interpretation of the sitter. This second type of portrait can be a purely subjective effort, and the task of such a study appears to be fulfilled so long as the photographer himself thinks that he has achieved what he set out to do.

In recent years we have seen a movement to get away from the classical approach to portraiture which was based on the photographer's analysis of his sitter and his ability to reproduce the result of his imaginative assessment in his picture.

The new approach, mainly pioneered by a few famous American photographers, is to rely more on the photo-journalist's approach than on that of the representational photographer. No doubt the use of electronic flash has much to do with this change of approach because instead of carefully coaxing and directing the sitter by word and action in front of the camera, many photographers now prefer to rely on instantaneous observation and the ability to "catch" the typical expression as it happens to occur. It must be made clear that both approaches have their obvious advantages and disadvantages.

114

It is obvious that the ordinary commercial portrait, aiming at creating a likeness which is appreciated not only by the sitter himself but also by his entire family, friends and relations, greatly restricts the photographer in his choice of lighting. He will definitely not make a success of his job if he "lights" a lady, who wishes to look twenty years younger, in such a way that she looks twenty years older, through employing hard spotlight effects, which meet the face at an oblique angle and bring all the wrinkles and skin texture in an exaggerated fashion. If he lights a gentleman who is very proud of his smart appearance, from underneath, so that he looks in a full-face view like an undernourished bulldog, he will also make himself unpopular. If, on the other hand, the photographer "sees" the gentleman in question as an undernourished bulldog and the aforementioned lady with the skin of a hippopotamus, and experiences the inner urge to announce these visions to the world, he is of course quite free to use lighting which emphasises those points. He should not be amazed, however—being an amateur and a relative of his models—if he is cut out from their wills or—being a professional photographer—if his "artistic" efforts are slammed round his ears.

It must be appreciated that, quite apart from questions of expediency, certain types of lighting are more suitable for profile, other types for full-face views, and I think that the reader will see best what can and cannot be done by basing the following examination not on the setting of the light sources, but on the various positions of the person to be photographed.

It is important to remember that the basic rules of lighting apply equally to monochrome and colour portraiture with the understanding that the permissible contrast ratio in colour photography is relatively restricted (see "Exposing colour materials", p. 67). For *conventional* colour portraiture it is essential to achieve an acceptable, naturalistic image and the "white" light used must be of a uniform colour temperature as dictated by the film stock used (see "Colour Balance", p. 22). For *character* studies, and particularly for *theatrical* work, this need not necessarily be so. In order to achieve dramatic, non-realistic effects, it is quite feasible to employ coloured light, produced by coloured gelatine filters in front of the light source by light of mixed colour temperature or coloured reflecting screens for the whole or part of the lighting scheme. In order to control the colour pattern it is obviously easier to use spot-lighting rather than flash for the main light source. When making portraits at home it is important to remember that light reflected from nearby surroundings will affect the colour image on the subject; although it is easy for the eye to overlook this incidental colour hue, the photographic emulsion will certainly show it clearly, often with disastrous effects.

THE PROFILE

A face seen in profile does not convey much actual expression. You see only one eye, and this only from a side view. The curve of the lips is only indicated, and the whole attitude of the sitter is turned away from the camera, and therefore also from the beholder of the picture.

A profile study is therefore only seldom suitable for bringing out the character of the person portrayed, and never suitable for establishing that certain kind of personal contact we so often perceive when a person looks at us. It can, however, help the photographer to bring out facial characteristics when these are to be found in the face's contour. Furthermore, that certain air of detachment intrinsic to the profile position can be utilised for creating certain ethereal facial effects.

Another advantage of a profile picture is that it often hides faults, thus flattering the sitter.

If we consider these main purposes of a profile picture, we can easily visualise the kind of lighting we have to employ in connection with the profile study. It will be obvious that if we wish to accentuate the outline of the face, we have to accentuate this outline by some means of lighting. There are two ways of doing this: either by a light contour against a darker background, or by a darker face-outline against a lighter background. The second method (dark outline against light background) is a rather old-fashioned mode and achieves a somewhat flat image of a two-dimensional character. The more modern method—accentuating the face's contour by means of a highlight—gives the photographer a better chance to modify the lighting according to his wishes and also lends itself to a greater variety of supplementary light effects.

Here are the main kinds of lighting treatment to be employed for a face in a full profile position.

Pure Silhouette

Especially suitable for "ghost" effects or any other occasions where the object of the illustration forbids the showing of realistic details.

Basic light: Floods on background only, creating a flat white tone all over.
Supplementary light: None.
Special remarks: It becomes apparent that by lighting the background only and leaving the object completely untouched by light, an extreme contrast of black and white is achieved. The effectiveness of a pure silhouette relies on a "telling" and easily distinguishable outline of the sitter.

116

THE PROFILE. Silhouettes are uncompromising pictures. They can be very characteristic with sitters of characteristic profiles. They can be made charming and witty by finding the appropriate pose. They do not, however, offer much variability in the lighting arrangements. Phot: *M. Salier, London.*

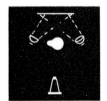

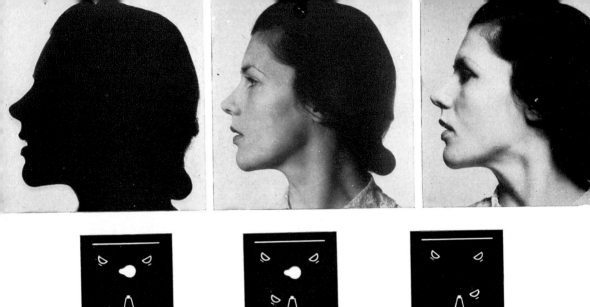

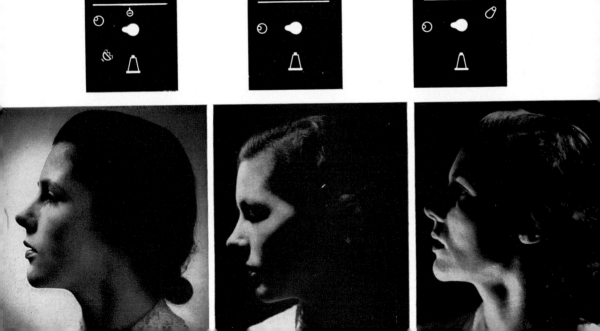

Top, from left to right: 1. Pure silhouette, *not* a silhouette shadow. Complete absence of light on the model. 2. Semi-silhouette, the basic lighting scheme of the pure silhouette supplemented by a flood standing left from the camera. 3. Dark outline profile: lighting similar to that for semi-silhouette but the supplementary flood now stands to the right of the camera, thus producing a dark rim along the facial contours. 4. Rim effect. Profile-outline accentuated by basic spot light which is supplemented by a flood, positioned as in the semi-silhouette treatment and by a diffused flood behind the model's head.

Bottom, from left to right: 1. Central light. Basic light produced by slightly elevated flood, causing small nose shadow on upper lip. Supplementary lighting: flood approximately half-way between basic light-source and camera and background light. 2. Top lighting. Basic light source in same position as in central lighting scheme but with much higher elevation. 3. Under lighting. Position of basic light source again as in the central-light scheme but here shining upon the model's face from below.

Page 119, from left to right: 1. Cross-light with dark background. Basic light from spot supplemented by another spot light behind the sitter's back so as to define the hair outline. 2. Same lighting scheme further supplemented by a flood so as to give detail to facial shadows. 3. Cross-light with light background. Basic light again from spot light. First supplementary light is the background illumination produced by a bare lamp standing behind model's head. Second supplementary light by frontal flood for shadow dilution.

On page 120, *top left*: Portrait Anton Walbrook. Normal central lighting. Flood produces dilution of the shadow parts. Phot: *Alexander, London. Top right*: Woollen worker. A straight-forward profile treatment, utilising cross-lighting for the main effect. A second spot was used to give the rim effect to the rear of the head; a diffused flood was used to render shadow detail. Phot: *W. Nurnberg. London. By courtesy of Hunt & Winterbotham. Right*: basic light is modified cross lighting produced by a spot. The supplementary light makes use of the ear to cast a pronounced light and shade pattern. The second supplementary light is a flood diluting the shadow slightly. Phot: *W. Nurnberg, London*.

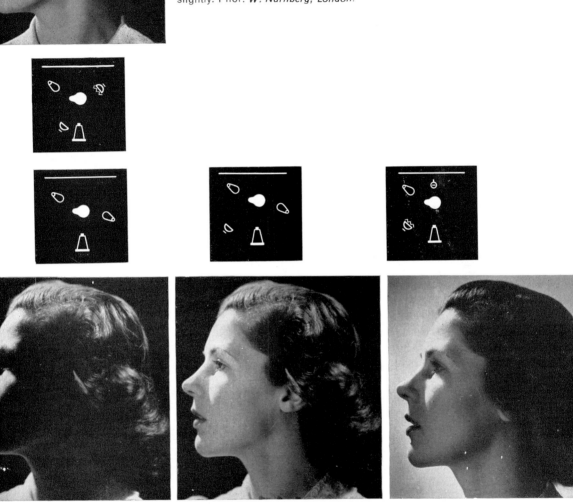

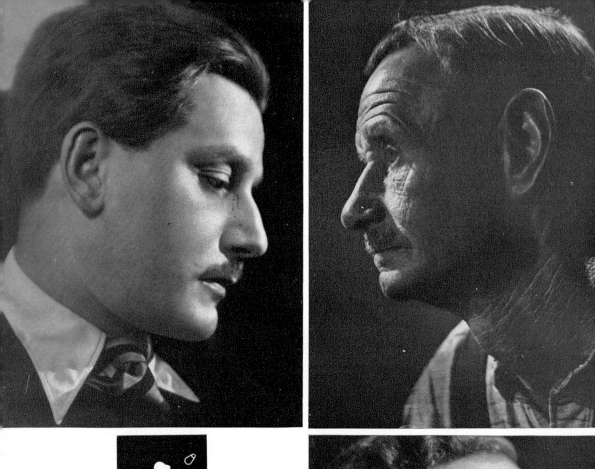

120

Suitable for ethereal effects in connection with the photography of young girls and women, also for "film star" effects in connection with male portraiture.

Basic light: Flood on background.
Supplementary Light: One diffused flood from near the camera but on the side which sitter is facing (side-lighting). Elevation of lamp the same as elevation of the head (level).
Second Supplementary Light: Can be employed for slightly "picking-up" dark hair. This should be done by a flood coming directly from the top, and must not touch the face of the sitter.
Special Remarks: It is obvious that the luminosity of the face must be less than the luminosity of the background. The tone value of the face is easily controlled by moving the lamp either nearer to or farther away from the sitter.

Dark-outline Lighting

An antiquated method still frequently used in commercial portrait studies. This kind of technique creates a very impersonal and flat effect which is without vigour and does not give the photographer scope for interpreting his own ideas. A dark outline profile can seldom go beyond producing a literal likeness.

Basic Light: Flood on background producing a white or grey tone.
Supplementary Light: Lamp position as that for semi-silhouette, but light source to be an *undiffused* flood. Hard lighting is an advantage and the light source could well be a flooded (slightly diffused) spotlight.
Special Remarks: The luminosity on the face produced by the supplementary light should equal approximately the luminosity on the background.

Rim Effect

Accentuating a well featured profile by means of a highlight along its contour. This lighting does not reach the nearside of the sitter's head and, if it is used without supplementary lighting, the effect will be very dramatic, although unsuitable for the creation of a likeness. If, on the other hand, a fill-in light for the shadows is added, this technique can be used for normal portrait work and character studies.

Basic Lighting: A spot-light is placed on the far side of the sitter at an elevation of approximately 45° and in such a position that no light touches the near cheek. (Side-lighting, medium elevation.)
Supplementary Light: For very dramatic effects: none. For lighting up near contour and hair: second spot-light from behind the sitter at a

121

high elevation; this spot-light should be more diffused than the one for the basic light.

Second Supplementary Light: Diffused flood of no elevation (level) flooding the shaded side of the face evenly. This lamp should be well away from the camera towards that side to which the sitter is looking (off-centre lighting, level).

Cross-light

This can be used for any kind of profile and, as we shall see later (see p. 132), also for three-quarter face and even full-face views. This particular light is called cross-light because a shadow is cast from the nose right across one side of the face in such a manner that this nose-shadow links up with the shadow of the cheek-bone. The light-and-shadow pattern thus created appears in the profile position as a rim light along the contours of the profile, at the same time producing a triangular light patch on the cheek facing the camera, and thus defining the line of cheek-bone.

In contrast to the four lighting treatments discussed above, this lighting aims at a three-dimensional effect by producing a very different pattern which defines the difference in perspective between front face and cheek. This lighting method is especially suitable for character work and men studies, but is not suited for use with a white background. Very deft and subtle effects can, however, be obtained if the shadows produced by the cross-lighting are lit up to approximately the same extent as the background; at the same time most masculine and powerful results are obtained by flooding the shadow parts of the face only slightly and using a black background.

Basic Light: Position similar to the one used for the rim effect. Here, however, the lamp is moved slightly forward so that not only the angle of elevation but the light incident upon the face are both approximately 45°. Thus the nose will cast a shadow upon the near cheek and, provided the lamp is in the correct position, there will be a marked triangular highlight on the face and the nose shadow will link fully with the massive shadow on the near-side of the head.

First Supplementary Light: Spot-light behind the head of sitter to produce rim-light effect on top and back of head.

Second Supplementary Light: Flood more or less diffused—beside the camera at an angle of 30° to the sitter's line of vision. This flood should not be elevated so that neither nose nor jaw cast shadows (off-centre lighting, level).

Third Supplementary Light: For background either flat-lighting to achieve an even all-over tone, or an effect whereby the side of the background which is behind the face of the sitter is kept in a low

122

key, gradually lightening to that side of the background which is behind the head of the sitter.

Special Remarks: I have suggested a spot-light as the light to be used for the basic light. My reason for this is that the whole idea of cross-lighting is based on a well-defined light-and-shadow pattern, and that a softening of the patterns edges would contradict the meaning of the cross-light. If necessary, quite satisfactory results can be obtained with a parabolic reflector fitted with a projector bulb.

Central Light

This type of light, when applied for full profile positions, aims at full illumination of the face, at the same time giving a very good rendering of the actual cheek-line by producing extensive plane and shadow at the side of the head. This light is usually used in connection with a black background and has no specific dramatic possibilities, but is very suitable for conventional portrait studies.

Basic Light: Flood (not diffused) placed in front of sitter's face, perhaps slightly towards the camera, elevation just high enough for the nose to cast a small shadow—which should not cover more than half of the upper lip.

First Supplementary Light: Diffused flood from level and a 30° lateral position exactly as the one used as second supplementary light for cross-lighting (p. 122).

Second Supplementary Light (Obligatory): Rim effect for top and back of head, as explained before, or soft top lighting to pick up dark hair from a dark background.

Special Remarks: We shall see presently that this type of light is very useful for three-quarter face, and especially for full-face positions where the variations in the elevation of the basic light achieve astonishing effects. Its usefulness for full profile pictures will be found limited because too long shadows must be avoided.

THE THREE-QUARTER FACE

To simplify classification I include in the term "three-quarter face" all the intermediary stages which lie between profile and full-face, such as the three-quarter, half, and quarter profile. It is only natural that, although each of these three positions may demand slight lighting adjustments, we have in principle always the same problems to solve. Three-quarter face positions are most frequently used in commercial portraiture. They offer the expressive possibilities of the full face but do not depend so much on either a classical profile contour or symmetrical features.

Obviously, a three-quarter face does not lend itself to the pure silhouette treatment, but, with this exception, the treatments already given for the profile are all suitable for three-quarter face lighting. It will be seen, however, that the lighting, although basically the same, is modified in details and consequently has a different role to play.

Semi-silhouette

Most suitable for soft feminine glamour where a slickness combined with emotion is aimed at. When photographing three-quarter faces the semi-silhouette treatment should always be used with supplementary lighting in order to add the necessary sparkle and lightness. In order to give the relieving highlights a chance, the tone of the background should be kept a light grey—not white. The tone of the sitter's face should be only slightly darker than the tone of the background.

Basic Light: Flood on background.
First Supplementary Light: Off-centre lighting, level, produced by a soft flood. The lamp position is at an angle of 30° to the sitter's line of vision, flooding the near-side of the sitter's head.
Second Supplementary Light: Spot-lighting from behind sitter so as to produce rim light on hair.
Special Remarks: A very effective method of treating the background in connection with half profile, and especially when subtle glamour effects are desired, is to create a halo of light around the head which quickly deteriorates towards its periphery. This *halo light can be achieved by placing a bare electric bulb behind the head of the sitter,* as near as possible to the background; another way of getting a similar but more contrasty effect is to project a halo of light on the background with a spot-light. If halo-lighting is used with a half-silhouette, the basic light will then be flat tone-lighting on the face and the halo will be composed around the subtly lighted form of the face.

Cross-light

In three-quarter face positions the cross-light is most useful; it can be projected on either side of the face with much variety of effect. If you look at Rembrandt's paintings you will find that cross-light effects have been predominantly used; also note that Rembrandt usually has the typical light triangle on the far side of the sitter's face. To copy this method in photography is dangerous because it entails a lighting which flattens the perspective of the whole side of the face near the camera; it also tends to unbalance composition by making the face look unsymmetrical. I therefore advise the use of cross-lighting in such a way that the shadow side of

124

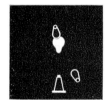

MORE THAN THE HEAD ONLY. *Left:* Portrait Sir Adrian Boult. Low key effect achieved by cross lighting. Although face and hands form only a comparatively small area of the picture, the accent which they receive from the two spot lights gives them the emphasis of a large-scale close-up. Phot: *Howard Coster, London.*

Right: Portrait Arthur Wontner. Modified double rim light giving emphasis again mainly to the head and hands. Phot: *Howard Coster, London.*

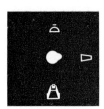

Portrait A. Kraszna-Krausz. Semi-silhouette with rim light effect both on profile and hands. Modified central light produced by baby spot. Phot: *Hugo van Wadenoyen Cheltenham.*

On page 127: Portrait G. K. Chesterton. A strong silhouette effect. Lighting on face is slightly modified. Normal central light. Phot: *Howard Coster, London.*

FASHION PHOTOGRAPHY. *On page* 128: the light effect on the background, the high elevation of the basic central light and the glamour shine on the hair achieved by a vigorous overhead spot, create a preponderance of dark tones with carefully placed high lights and a general impression of richness and warmth. Phot: *W. Maywald, Paris.*

On page 129: a brilliantly simple lighting scheme making use of the reflecting properties of the book in the model's hands. Phot: *K. Schenker, London.*

On page 130: A dance study of strongly emotional character. Basic effect produced by elevated and modified rim lighting and supplemented by a further rim light on the lower part of the figure. Phot: *F. S. Lincoln, New York.*

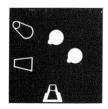

On page 131: Contrasty lighting and concentrated expressions help to tell the story of these Men of Steel. Phot: *W. Nurnberg, London (by courtesy of United Steel Companies).*

On page 132: Study in a High-Key Mood. The main lighting is on the background which reflects back on to the figure. Soft conventional fill-in is added to give a soft feminine appeal. Phot: *Norman Parkinson, London (by courtesy of Vogue).*

On page 133: Dramatic Male Fashion. High-Contrast, modified side-lighting against shaded background renders textures well and creates dynamic impression. Phot: *Norman Eales, London (by courtesy of Vogue).*

On page 134: Group. An unusual amount of lighting was necessary to create exposure conditions (1/100 sec. at *f*11) for a candid shot. Phot: *W. Nurnberg, London.*

On page 136: The symmetrical character of the double rim lighting stresses the quiet atmosphere and composition. Phot: *W. Nurnberg, London (by courtesy of J. Tate & Partners).*

On page 137: Nude with body emphasis. Semi-silhouette effect relieved by rim light and top light. Modelling and warmth have not been sacrificed, and yet crudeness has been avoided. Phot: *U. Lang–Kurz, Stuttgart.*

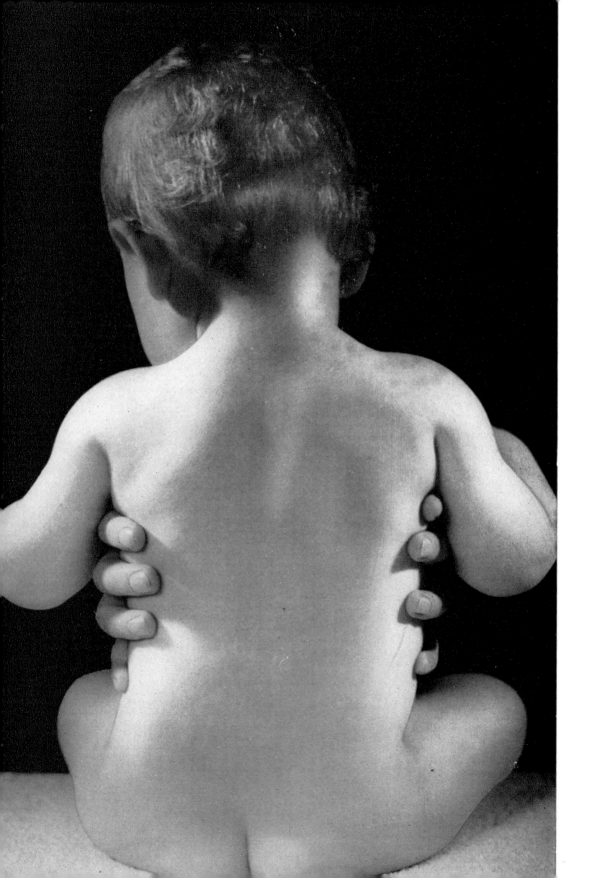

Left: the front figures are lit by separate units. The rim effects on each of them are produced by the two basic light sources, while the background figure gets its illumination by the general flood and overhead lighting only. Phot: *K. Schenker, London.*

Right: an under-angle shot of strong diagonal composition emphasised by rim lighting on man's head and arm. The girl is lit individually by cross lighting method and a separate hair light from the back. The paper in the foreground is also lit separately by diffused flood, assisted by a second flood for general lighting of the whole subject. Phot: *W. Nurnberg (by courtesy of J. Haddon & Co. Ltd.).*

HANDS AND FEET. *Opposite:* simplest possible treatment for lighting a hand. Phot: *Ifor Thomas, London.*
On page 140, top left: basic light produced by a top-angle spot, supplemented by very diffused front lighting. Phot: *Sougez, Paris.*
Top right: the hands lit by two spot lights of great intensity to get short exposure times. Phot: *W. Nurnberg, London (by courtesy of John Tate & Partners). Right:* simple modelling by a complicated light scheme. Phot: *W. Nurnberg, London.*

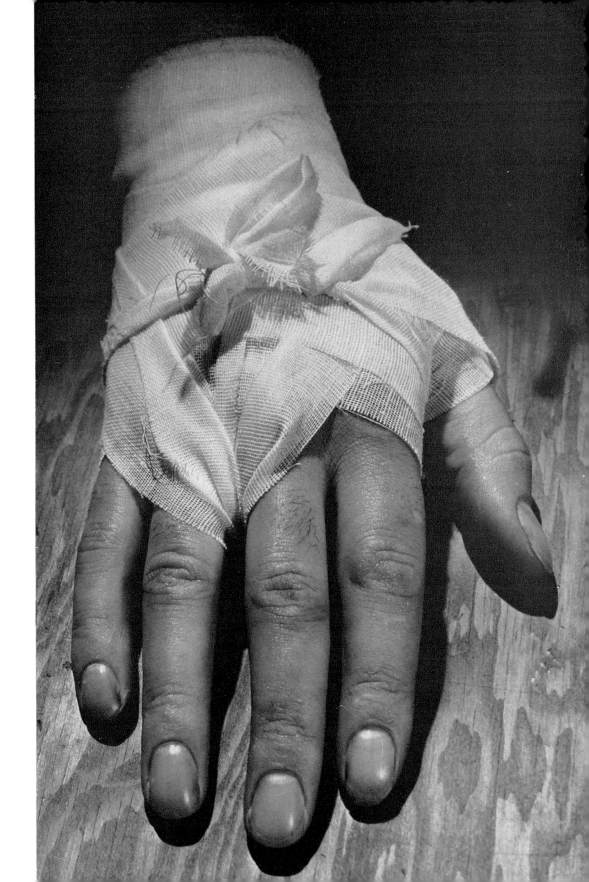

140

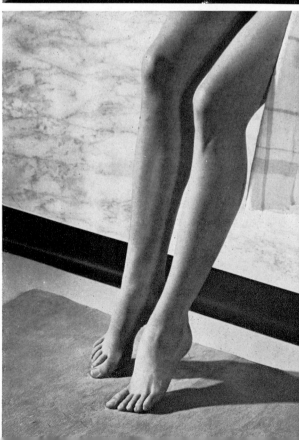

the face faces the lens. The far side of the sitter's face become better balanced by the small light triangle. The extensive shadow area on the near side of the face can be balanced by creating a dark background behind the far side of the face.

Basic Light: Spot-light of the kind already explained. The actual position naturally depends on the position of the head and of the light triangle (near or far side of the face).
First Supplementary Light: Spot-light behind the head of sitter to produce rim-light effect on top and back of head. In male portraiture this supplementary light can be slightly modified to obtain an interesting effect. If this spot-light, giving a rim on the back and top of the head, is moved very slightly away from the direction of the background, a rim of light can also be produced along the lower jaw. Care must be taken, however, not to break up the compact shadow masses intrinsic to the cross-light technique.
Second Supplementary Light: Flood, more or less diffused at an elevation which eliminates the casting of a nose shadow.
Special Remarks: I prefer to use cross-lighting for three-quarter faces on dark backgrounds, but this lighting can equally well be applied to any tone of background.

Side-light

I recommend the use of the side-light, particularly for the three-quarter face position, especially if it is applied to that side of the face which lies away from the camera. Side-lighting is particularly effective for three-quarter faces against a black background. The position for the basic light source is on the far side of the sitter at an elevation of approximately 45°. The lamp should be so placed that only the far side of the face is lighted, whilst the near cheek is not reached by light. In other words, the effect is that the side of the face beyond the nose is fully lighted, while the other side—facing the camera—is in shadow. Side-lighting is most suitable for character studies and can be combined with a number of interesting supplementary lighting effects.

Side-lighting used for full-face portraiture is also effective on light backgrounds, particularly for the portraiture of women.

Basic Light:
(1) For dark background: lamp position as explained above, elevation: lamp at the height of top of sitter's head. The most suitable light source is a parabolic flood or diffused spot-light.
(2) For light background: the most suitable light source would be diffused flood, electronic flash, or indirect bounced lighting.

L   141

First Supplementary Light: Spot-light from back of sitter at a high elevation, throwing the ear-shadow downwards; the lamp must be moved just far enough forward (in the direction of the camera) for the side-face of the sitter to be vigorously lighted, thus creating texture and a very good definition of the cheek-bone and jaw line.

Second Supplementary Light: More or less diffused flood-lamp from off-centre level on the near-side of the face, as explained before for the first supplementary lighting for the semi-silhouette. This light will lighten the shadows without altering the basic effect.

Special Remarks: I wish to repeat again that this lighting is particularly masculine. Many other supplementary light positions can be found for this treatment, and certain modifications which, explained in detail, would lead too far.

Central Light

Most applicable to half-profile positions. It has enormous possibilities for not only altering the character of the picture, but also for completely changing the look of the face itself. This is all the more amazing as central lighting is very straightforward. As its name implies, it always shines, more or less, "right in front of the sitter's nose". The amazing changes I have mentioned are obtained merely by altering the elevation of the lamp.

If the central light is brought high overhead, the forehead, nose, lower lip and cheek-bones give long and heavy shadows; thus high central lights are ideal for depression and headache pictures.

By shifting the basic lamp lower, we get the ordinary conventional kind of lighting—namely, that which produces a small shadow, more or less symmetrical, underneath the nose, with good definition of lips, eyes and cheeks. This kind of lighting is adequate if one wishes to keep the picture in a conventional mood.

By bringing the basic lamp still lower, until the nose shadow disappears, the face becomes very flat; lips, forehead, part of the face and the chin region are very badly defined.

This third modification of the central light is really useful only when deliberately depersonalising a face. It gives some kind of ethereal quality to a half-profile when used in connection with light backgrounds and supplementary glamour lighting originating from behind the sitter.

The fourth modification of the central light is also called under-light. As the light source is placed under chin-level of the sitter, the face takes on a demoniac appearance. Usually one does not consciously perceive the visual effect of under-lighting, although we ought to be accustomed to it from the homely fireplace or the foot-lights of the stage, but it is a fact that every time one looks at a picture, especially a close-up picture, in which all shadows are

142

cast upwards one associates it with a somewhat Mephistophelian atmosphere.

Basic Light: This depends very much on the length and direction of the facial shadows. The reader can best compare methods of lamp-positioning and effects when looking at the pictures and diagrams. It is still better if he makes his own experiments. The basic light should normally be produced by a flood, but a spot-light can be substituted for it when very well-defined shadows are desired.

Supplementary Lights: Their main task here is to relieve the shadows and give extra definition to the top and the back of the sitter's head or, if so desired, give further illumination to the background. The main supplementary light—*i.e.* the one relieving the depth of shadow —should always be placed on that side of the camera facing the sitter. The elevation of the lamp producing this light should always be low enough to avoid new shadows. Its sole purpose is to relieve existing shadows—not to create new ones.

THE FULL FACE

The full-face position in portraiture demands a good face. The human face seen absolutely from the front can, from the point of view of composition, be considered an extremely symmetrical form. If the natural symmetry of the face is disturbed by faults of the face itself, such as "spoon-ears" or "sword-noses", this may be very interesting to the physiologist, or even to the photographic student, but I am sure the model to whom that face belongs will not be too pleased at having his shortcomings accentuated and memorised in a photograph. It is for this reason that, as mentioned before, three-quarter face positions (or at least positions which are just off the full-face angle) are usually employed in commercial portraiture.

Symmetrical lighting accentuates facial symmetry, and it is for this reason that all forms of central-lighting are predominantly employed for full-face positions. But cross-lighting can also find useful application. Besides these two there is a new method of lighting—the "double-rim light".

Central Light

Here, as in connection with half profiles, the central light gives to the photographer a wealth of latitude in the free moulding of form and in the infusion into his picture of a wide range of different sensorial qualities. Again it is the elevation of the light-source which brings forth the various pictorial and psychological changes; it is in the full-face position that under-lighting can be most usefully employed.

143

Basic Light: For top lighting: light source as near as possible to lens of camera. For normal position (*i.e.* small nose shadow): approximately the same light position as above. For extreme cases of top- and under-lighting: the light-source should be placed as near as possible either above the head or below the chin, thus creating the desired shadows without the lamp itself being in the field of camera-vision.

Supplementary Light: Produced by flood-lighting, diffused spherical reflectors being preferable. Position of supplementary light: one flood lamp on each side of camera somewhere half-way between camera and sitter, but not too near the sitter. It should be watched that these floods are not producing new shadows in the face, and it might for this reason be safer to substitute the two front lamps by paper reflectors which give a softer light.

Second Supplementary Light: It can be employed from right overhead, thus giving definition in the sitter's hair and creating a well-defined shoulder outline.

Special Remarks: It should be remembered that a central-light in connection with a full-face position has the important task of accentuating the symmetrical form of the face and of creating a symmetrical light-and-shadow pattern, though such rules must not be taken too literally. This symmetry of the face can be departed from by shifting the central light slightly out of the central axis if one has a good reason and justification for departing from the orthodox way of lighting.

Double-rim Light

The double-rim light is a special full-face lighting. We have already made its acquaintance without having called it by its proper name, *i.e.* in the rim-lighting method applied to a profile picture where the light produced a second rim along the back of the head. I did not mention that this lighting had a double-rim light, because it was then merely a variation of the ordinary rim effect which could be applied or not. Now, in the full-face position the double-rim light becomes a lighting scheme in itself. The reason for this is again the symmetry of the full face, which makes a one-sided rim-lighting appear out of balance. This double-rim light is the one exception where the basic light is constructed by two lamp sources instead of one. The use of the double-rim light should be confined to slim faces; fat cheeks would be extraordinarily exaggerated by this type of lighting. It is ideal for glamour effects, and lends dramatic value to the picture when used in conjunction with a black background. It creates very subtle "pastel" effects when used with a light grey or light medium grey background. It is obvious that the double-rim light is a lighting method which never consists of a basic light alone. It always needs the addition of some kind of supplementary light.

Basic Light: Two spot-lights, one on each side slightly behind the sitter in a position which creates an outline on each side of the face without the light-beam touching the tip of the nose. Flood-lamps should not be employed, because they would shine too easily into the lens and lead to flare.

Supplementary Light: The most suitable supplementary light for this double-rim lighting is a completely frontal light; a diffused flood should for this reason be placed as near to the lens as possible, its elevation being low enough not to cast a nose shadow. This supplementary light can be modified if there should be any reason to do so, but any adjustment should be made by changing the elevation of the lamp, *i.e.* shifting it perpendicularly rather than horizontally.

Special Remarks: The double rim-lighting can also be used as *supplementary effect* to other lighting schemes—especially in connection with central lighting.

Cross-light

I think that one can say that the character of the cross-light contradicts the character intrinsic to the form created by a full-face position. At the same time, this divergence in character can very often be the means of achieving not only outstanding pictorial effects, but of conveying a certain restlessness or any unusual characteristics of the sitter. The use of cross-lighting in connection with a full-face position should therefore be strictly reserved for special purposes, and not be degraded by use without thought or purpose on every humdrum occasion.

Basic Light: The position of the lamps in relation to the face of the sitter has already been explained in detail.

Supplementary Light: Again the main supplementary light is one for lightening the shadows to any desired degree. The photographer must watch that this lamp produces no new shadow anywhere on the face. The best method of avoiding such lapses is to place a more or less diffused flood-lamp as near as possible to the line of camera-vision (*i.e.* as near as possible to the lens), at an elevation which does not produce a visible shadow; the lamp should, however, be placed on the side of the lens facing the shadow side of the sitter's face.

LIGHTING A FIGURE

Lighting for figure work is nothing but an extension of that kind of lighting we already know from portraiture. It is therefore imperative

145

that the beginner should not attempt to tackle figure studies before he has mastered the lighting of a face. This is so much easier than the lighting of a figure, because each face presents about the same principal problems of lighting. A figure, on the other hand, requires a new and individual approach every time. While the head is a more or less static form, a figure changes its appearance most radically with every movement. Furthermore, a nude confronts us with an entirely different proposition from a dressed figure. To make matters even more complicated we have to decide if we are to photograph its full length or only a part of it. We cannot assess the number of different combinations of lighting, but we can form a few standard rules which form the basis for successful figure lighting.

The Nude

The lighting of a figure in the nude can be treated from two main aspects. We can aim either at a soft and delicate high-key image or at a warm and sensuous image achieved by broad areas of light and shadow and added effect lights.

I am not going to discuss the "pros and cons" of the different schools of thought; it is all very much a matter of personal attitude towards this particular subject. It should be realised, however, that the lack of deep shadow areas requires a perfect body, because no blemish of shape or detail can be hidden under a veil of darkness.

Whichever type of style is decided upon the basic technical approach must always be the same namely that the basic light has to be well established first and the effect carefully studied. Only after a satisfactory anatomical representation has been achieved by the first light should the supplementary lighting be added and built up.

Whenever we wish to stress the roundness and softness of a body, the basic light source should also be soft. If direct lighting is used the elevation of the basic lamp should be such that it renders the anatomical structure of the body without exaggerating it. Shadows must therefore be placed so that they fall naturally, and consequently show the form of the body truly. The supplementary lighting can either be a rim highlight produced by a spot accentuating the various features of the body, or a flood diluting the shadows produced by the basic light—or both.

When photographing a nude "full-face", we can also use the double-rim lighting, in which case the basic light is produced by two symmetrically placed spots.

Nude profiles can be well treated as silhouettes or half-silhouettes.

The Dressed Figure

The Dressed Figure gives us again different problems which vary with monochrome and colour photography and these are made even

146

more complex by the fact that dressed figures are photographed for different reasons all of which may require a different lighting approach.

First, full length figure portraiture has become recently more fashionable as many portraitists have become increasingly concerned with spontaneity of action besides that of facial expression.

Second, full-length figure studies are used increasingly in consumer advertising.

Third, full-length figures are a natural part of most industrial subjects.

Fourth, the fashion photographer is obviously concerned more than anybody else with this particular subject.

Generally, shadowless photography should be avoided in the monochrome treatment of dressed figures, particularly when used in the fashion and industrial fields. Flat lighting is unsuitable to show detail and texture. In colour photography this is not necessarily true as the colour-contrast of the garments will enhance the visual realisation of both anatomic structures and design. It is also obvious that the lighting scheme will depend much on the design of a garment and the posture of the body. A standing figure in a trouser suit can do with less detailed contour lighting than one wrapped in the soft fold-pattern of a garment, and so on.

Keeping the above generalities in mind, here are a few hints:

When photographing a figure slightly sideways, the side should be kept darker than the front; otherwise we not only get a flat and shapeless image, but also render the figure much too wide.

A figure photographed from the front (which should be posed not rigidly but in a soft elongated *S* shape) should be lit by a kind of cross-lighting or rim or even double-rim lighting so as to accentuate the curves and, consequently, the action of the body.

The building up of figure-lighting can now be done in two principal ways. Firstly, we can light the head and shoulders, and then add the lighting necessary for the body, or *vice versa*. This first way will usually be employed by the amateur who does not possess lamps which emit a light-beam of a width sufficient to cover an upright standing figure, or to illuminate the total extent of the figure. The second way—open to the professional—is to employ light sources big enough to create a basic light for the whole of the figure (including head and shoulders). But even he will find it often useful to *light the head separately from the body*; this applies especially when he has to deal with a dark garment which needs a much longer exposure time than the face, or whenever he may wish to render the face and bare shoulders as a semi-silhouette while the garment is presented in full and plastic light. These considerations play an important part in fashion photography. While some differentiation of lighting for

147

face and figure is quite permissible, an excessive and unnatural differentiation, tending to divide the picture into two separately lit components, should be avoided.

Another important problem in connection with figure photography is the lighting of the background. When dealing with a realistic setting, such as the wall of a room, the lighting scheme will be obvious. Kitchen or "sunny-room" backgrounds need "general flood"; but "evening interiors" or gruesome cellar surroundings call for subdued and eerie effects which are usually obtained by angle spot-lighting or cast shadow effects on the background.

The issue becomes more involved if we choose a plain background on which to "paint" an abstract light-and-shadow pattern in order to create a certain atmosphere. Here the lighting of the background element becomes just as important as the lighting on the figure itself. The background takes on a life of its own, a life which must supplement the realism of the foreground with an abstract quality. This kind of background lighting depends firstly on the use of tones or colour, and secondly on shapes. The shapes are determined by the kind of lamp and the angle of light incidence (here our knowledge of the bogus shadow comes in most handy see p. 99). The tone is determined by supplementary lighting which controls the extent of dilution of the dark areas.

Whatever kind of background treatment we wish to apply to figures, it is essential that we keep the figure well away from the background. An exception to the rule is permitted on those occasions where the pictorial theme demands a cast and annexed shadow from the object on the background.

HINTS ON THE LIGHTING OF GROUPS

We have to distinguish between portrait groups (head and shoulders) and figure groups. There is one principle valid for both, namely that *a group is one unit*. This means that the lighting must be such that the unit is not disturbed and torn apart by disconnected patches of light and shadow. In other words, the lighting must connect the individual figures with each other—not separate them! In order to achieve this, any lighting scheme for groups must be thought out and not arrived at haphazardly.

In detail lighting, technique varies greatly according to the make-up of a group.

When dealing with *small figure groups* (one or two figures close together), our best approach is to use one basic light, preferably from a large spot-light or large electronic flash-head. In this way each of the figures will be illuminated equally, although the effect on each of the figures will be a different one provided the figures differ

148

THREE-QUARTER FACE. The dark outline profile technique is an unorthodox treatment for three-quarter face and should be used with care. Not every face can stand up to the over-emphasised foreshortening of the side away from the camera and to the resulting accentuation of the nose line. Phot: *Eric Balg, Berlin.*

Top: Semi-silhouette. Basic light is the background illumination. First supplementary light: flood left from the camera, elevation such as to avoid cast shadows on the face and to give the face a slightly darker tone than that of the background. Second supplementary light: spot light from behind the sitter for hair lighting. *Bottom:* The three types of central lighting. *Left:* Normal central light. Basic light: frontal flood slightly elevated. First supplementary light: spot from behind the sitter. Second supplementary light: background illumination produced by a bare lamp behind the model. Third supplementary light: flood near the basic light source at an elevation which avoids further cast shadows on the face. *Centre:* Top-lighting. Basic light: highly elevated central light. First supplementary light: spot for hair definition as before. Second supplementary light: frontal flood for shadow diffusion. *Right:* Under-lighting. Basic light: central lighting from a very low angle, supplemented by a back-spot.

On page 151, *top:* Two types of cross-light treatment. *Left:* Light-triangle pointing towards camera. Basic light in orthodox lamp position supplemented by a spot and a frontal flood. *Right:* light-triangle pointing towards background. Basic light produced by

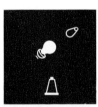

spot near the camera. First supplementary light: back-spot. Second supplementary light: background illumination. Third supplementary light: frontal flood for shadow diffusion.

Bottom: Side-lighting. *Left:* One-sided side-lighting: basic lighting by spot illuminating far side of model's face. First supplementary light: back-spot. Second supplementary light: frontal flood, lighting up the near side of the face. Third supplementary light: background illumination. *Right:* Double side lighting.

Basic light as before by spot. First supplementary light: elevated spot-light illuminating the cheek facing the camera and accentuating the cheek bone. Second supplementary light: frontal flood; third supplementary light: background illumination.

On page 152, *top left:* double side lighting. Phot: *W. Nurnberg, London (by courtesy of Alfred Pemberton, Ltd.).* Top right: cross light treatment supplemented by rim light on back and top of head. Light treatment of background. Phot: *W. Nurnberg, London (by courtesy of John Haddon & Co.).* Right: semi-silhouette individualised by a cleverly set rim high light. Light on the background. Phot: *Hugo van Wadenoyen, Cheltenham.*

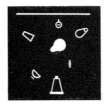

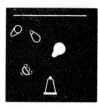

152

THE FULL FACE. *Top left:* cross-light produced by 45-degree spot lighting. First supplementary light: back-spot for hair definition. Second supplementary light: frontal flood for shadow diffusion (omitted in diagram). *Top right:* Double rim-lighting. Basic light produced by two spots resulting in symmetrical light rim around the face. Supplementary light: frontal flood avoiding cast shadows.

Bottom: Central lighting. *Left:* normal central light. Basic light produced by slightly elevated flood causing small nose shadow. First supplementary light: background illumination. Second supplementary light produced by a flat reflector for shadow diffusion. *Centre:* Top-lighting. Basic light produced by strongly elevated flood. First supplementary light: background illumination. Second supplementary light: frontal flood. *Right:* Under lighting. Basic light: directed to the face from a very low angle. Supplementary light by two spots symmetrically placed behind the model's head, achieving halo-effect.

Portrait Barbara Stanwyck. Normal central lighting assisted by overhead lighting. Phot: *Hurrell, Hollywood.*
Opposite: The simplicity of a master photographer's lighting schemes, which achieve so much with so little, is again demonstrated. The basic lighting is a simple side light, supplemented by a frontal flood. Phot: *Hurrell, Hollywood.*

On page 156, *top left:* dramatic effect by underlighting. Phot:
H. von Perkhammer, Berlin. Top right: similar dramatic appearance
of unusually cast shadows achieved by top lighting. Phot: *Cyril
Arapoff, Oxford. Right:* Portrait Andre Simon. Double rim lighting,
supplemented by flood from front and diffused flood on the background. Phot: *W. Nurnberg, London (by courtesy of Mather &
Crowther).*

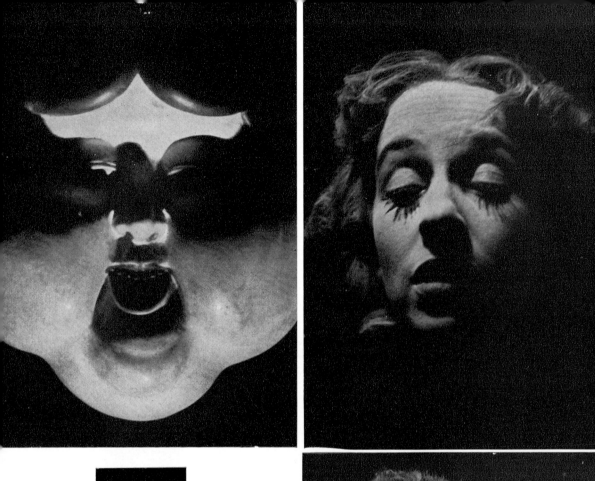

in their position. To give just one example: in a group one figure faces us full face, whilst a second figure to the left of the first is in a three-quarter position. One lamp is placed sideways on the right. The effect will be to give the full-face a side-light effect, whilst the three-quarter face will be more fully lighted by either a cross-lighting or off-centre lighting.

In order to light such a group as one unit the lamp itself must have sufficient "throw" from some considerable distance; a 2-kW fresnel lens spot-light is the ideal light-source for such a purpose. To lighten the shadows of a small group, one large general flood unit is usually sufficient. Additional highlight effects can then be added, using small spot-lights in the orthodox way. Similarly, a direct, strong electronic flash-unit may be used for the main light while the fill-in lighting can now be provided by general, bounced light or, directly, by a weaker, possibly diffused, electronic unit.

When dealing with *large figure groups* (three persons or more placed somewhat apart from each other) a more complicated lighting technique is unavoidable. The main lighting will now have to be produced by at least two spot-lights. One we shall use again to light two of the figures which are nearest to each other. If this first lamp has a wide enough spread, it can be used to give *back-lighting* to the third person simultaneously. The second main lamp will likewise light the backs of the two other figures whilst producing the main lighting on the third and fourth figures. If the figures are particularly far apart from each other, the use of a third spot-light may be essential. Although two 2-kW spot-lights may be considered essential for this large light build-up, the third need hardly ever be bigger than a 500-watt spot-light.

With three basic light-sources giving different effects, it is not easy to lighten all shadows evenly. Again, the ideal is to use one large general flood. In a well-equipped commercial studio this should not be a problem as the necessary flood-lighting can be supplied by large overhead flood aggregates. On location, on the other hand, where small flood reflectors are used, the supplementary fill-in lighting must be handled with great care in order to avoid cross shadows and confusing highlights.

With high-powered flash leads giving a broad area of high-level illumination the matter of lighting a large group seems at first sight very much simpler. The danger here is that one can make life a little too simple by using the broad and powerful flash illumination to merely "light out" the subject without any real attempt to imbue the scene and the individual personalities with that character and expression which shows up the difference between a picture made by a good, imaginative photographer and that by a competent hack.

Lastly, we come to the lighting of *Portrait Groups.* Here lighting is obviously much simpler because we rarely photograph more than two sitters, and these are always placed near to each other. Moreover, not having to take "figure" into account, we can approach the problem purely from a portrait lighting point of view. The simple equipment recommended for portraiture will suffice (see page 59).

It is, obviously, outside the scope of a general textbook to go into the detail of lighting schemes for groups of which there are literally hundreds of variations. A few general principles must, therefore, suffice. Figures which are lighted by cross-lighting will be more forceful and conspicuous than those given a more symmetrical, central lighting. We thus can emphasise a figure in the background by giving it a type of light which demands more attention than the light used on the more dominating foreground figures. We can obviously reverse this example and subdue a figure in the background still further either by rendering it darker or by accentuating the foreground units by a more interesting play of light and shadow. If it is desired to emphasise one particular figure within a group, it is easy to give this figure an additional effect-light (such as a rim-light) whilst the other figures remain lighted in a simple, straightforward manner.

I wish to repeat here that accentuation by additional highlight effect must on no account be overdone; otherwise we shall obtain just those patchy effects which must in all circumstances be avoided.

Always bear in mind that, especially in portraiture, the accentuating supplementary highlight effect on individual figure must conform with their individual characters. It will not do to light a male figure with a glamorous double-rim lighting while its female counterpart is treated with a masculine cross-lighting or even by under-lighting.

Let us never forget that lighting is not only a means of illumination but also a means of characterisation. Therefore, if it is a purpose of a group picture to demonstrate similarity of character, the figures in a portrait group should be given a similar, if not the same type of, lighting (not necessarily by only one light-source). If, however, it is the aim to demonstrate differences of character each figure should be given its own appropriate lighting.

Group lighting is by its very nature always a rather complex affair, and it is, therefore, all the more important to construct the lighting schemes systematically and accurately. The simpler the lighting the more will it help to create a homogeneous image and convey harmony between the individual units of the picture.

THE LIGHTING OF HANDS

The lighting of hands depends to a great extent on the movement and individual position of the hand, and it is therefore difficult to set

158

up rules which would cover this particular branch of photography systematically. There is hardly another field requiring more personal experience and open-mindedness from the photographer. One must not cling too tightly to preconceived ideas. At the same time, there are a number of rules which are generally applicable.

First we have to consider if we have to photograph an outstretched hand or a fist. The shallow form of an *outstretched hand demands a soft basic lighting* which—supplemented with a few carefully placed highlights—gives good modelling. A *fist calls for a contrasty spot-lighting* which dissects the form of the hand into distinct areas of light and shadow and which makes the bend of the fingers and the typical three-dimensional character of the fist clearly perceptible.

We then have to take into account whether the hands are closely connected with a background—consequently casting annexed shadows—or whether they are detached from the background so that the background shadows can be isolated and shifted outside the field of camera-vision.

It is obvious that hands which are far away from a background can be lighted much more effectively than those near a background. The proximity of a background—being nearly always in the way of the lamps—makes, indeed, many light variations impossible. One of the most dramatic and appropriate methods of lighting for an outstretched hand is, for instance, the double-rim light, but, as we have seen in the portrait section, this particular lighting is based on an acute angle of light incidence, only to be achieved by having the object well away from the background.

You will find that you have to be most careful in the choice of the camera-angle in order to avoid optical distortions (especially watch bent fingers, which tend to be easily foreshortened). Inappropriate lighting will emphasise these distortions. For instance: if you light a hand in front of a black background in such a way that the fore-shortened link of a finger is in "shadow", then the distortion will be stressed. This, however, does *not* imply that distortions should be rectified by playing about with the lighting; to rectify these faults we have to go back to their source, *i.e.* alter the position of either the hand or the camera.

Another fact determining the choice of lighting is the object of the picture. Hands of men—especially in connection with industrial work or any other kind of manual labour—should be treated with vigorous spot-light effects which stress the exertion of power and energy. Women's hands obviously demand an entirely different treatment. Here the image must be glamorous and uncomplicated, and it follows that flood-lighting will play a more prominent part.

It is obvious that the photography of hands demands precision lighting and thus we must have complete control over the lighting

159

equipment. Flash techniques are generally unsuitable and a simple incandescent lighting outfit (as recommended for portraiture) is always the better choice. The use of one or two low-angle brackets for the 500-W spot-lights will be found particularly useful here. Also, as hands are generally lighted from relatively nearby the use of diffuser screens is important in controlling the balance of tones and contrast.

LIGHT AND SHADOW
AS APPLIED TO THE INANIMATE

Under the heading of this chapter falls everything usually described as still-life photography or "reproduction". These two terms cover the photography of everything from flat originals to the most intricate groupings of three-dimensional matter. My object here is to investigate the problems of still-life photography from the lighting viewpoint only.

We have to tackle this wide field systematically, and must therefore first draft a plan of campaign. The first and simplest step is the reproduction of flat originals; next, the reproduction of surfaces which are light-absorbent; thirdly, the reproduction of predominantly reflecting surfaces.

THE REPRODUCTION OF FLAT ORIGINALS

Some professional photographers do nothing but reproduce flat originals, such as black-and-white drawings, oil paintings, etc. Also belonging to this class of work is the reproduction of fabrics in the flat, as used for catalogue illustrations. The beginner very often tends to underestimate the difficulties connected with this "straightforward" photographic process.

The problems of lighting of this kind of work can roughly be summed up in one sentence: *The light sources must be placed so that they illuminate the surface evenly and completely, and so that the material being photographed does not produce concentrated reflections.* This basic rule applies to both monochrome and colour.

Firms specialising in photographic reproduction work have often to use a variety of intricate apparatus, for they have not only to produce an image which is evenly lighted, but one which—in black and white photography—reproduces colours in the tones of the

161

monochromatic scale which have either to represent fairly the colours of the original, or which are purposely faked. The professional black-and-white photographer has all the necessary filters at his disposal to do both, but the amateur will obtain good results with the help of the following suggestions:

(1) Use as light sources spherical reflectors and frosted bulbs only.

(2) Never put lamps in such a position that the incident light meets the surface perpendicularly, in other words, place them sideways. Also note that it is imperative that each lamp produces a light of the same efficiency, and that they are placed at the same distance from *and* absolutely symmetrically about the flat surface to be reproduced.

(3) For not too large areas two flood-lamps are adequate. For larger propositions four flood-lights may be required.

(4) In conjunction with tungsten filament light the amateur will find a set of filters necessary; deep yellow, dark orange, medium red and green will usually cover his requirements.

(5) The colour reproduction of coloured flat originals presents less difficulties, provided that the colour temperature of the light is correct and all extraneous incidental lighting is excluded. Do not forget to switch off the room light and darken the windows and also avoid reflected light from nearby walls and ceiling, or from furniture placed too near.

RENDERING TEXTURES

Texture rendering is essentially a matter of lighting. Even if we admit the importance of other considerations, such as camera-technique and the object-arrangement, we cannot get round the fact that the rendering of textures stands or falls by the right application of light. This is just as valid in colour photography as it is in mono-chrome. We shall be more successful in our aim if the surface to be photographed does not reflect light excessively. Needless to say, we cannot pick up texture where there is none, as in transparent or purely reflective surfaces, but neither must we assume that a light-absorbing surface always lends itself easily to texture rendering. We have seen, for instance (p. 29), that black velvet absorbs approximately 99·7% of the incident light—yet it is almost impossible to represent black velvet successfully by means of photography.

We want a surface which is rough enough to become, under the influence of light, a pattern of minute highlight and shadow particles. It is obvious that *the shallower are the "bumps" constituting the texture of the surface, the more oblique must be the angle of incident light.*

162

Furthermore, it is obvious that *the harder the light, the more pronounced will be the surface-impression of light and shadow;* the reason being the perfected definition of the shadow parts.

Fabrics

Texture is not everything which counts in a fabric and which is characteristic of it. Pattern, for example is often neglected in black-and-white photography; especially in woven fabrics, texture is forced to a point of sacrificing pattern completely.

This also can apply to colour photography when dealing with self-coloured fabrics; with multi-coloured patterns this problem is, of course, less acute.

Fabric photography is not "art", nor is it usually done merely for fun; mostly it is produced for advertising purposes—for the purpose of selling goods. Therefore the photographer has no right to exaggerate texture in a photographic image when the fabric does not demand it. On the other hand, photographers who have not the ability to make good texture photographs should not excuse their failing by saying that they were reproducing some insignificant pattern when the fabric demanded a bold texture treatment.

It has been already mentioned (above) that the more one wishes to force a texture the more oblique must be the angle at which the light falls upon the surface, and that the extent of light diffusion determines the extent of texture rendering. If we could look upon the rendering of a fabric's surface as the only task of a fabric photograph, things would be easy. Having a piece of fabric lying on a table, and placing the carbon spot-light nearly as low as the height of the table, so that the light-beam just touches the fabric on the table, we shall observe (especially if we view this "scene" more or less against the light) that we obtain a tremendous roughness—probably an exaggerated roughness. We could then try to amend this basic lighting by using a very diffused flood to soften the contrast. Or we can choose another way—by elevating the basic light source to produce shorter-texture shadows, and thus a less exaggerated effect. As a third alternative, we can use for our basic light source, not a carbon spot-light, but a light of softer quality, *e.g.* a diffused filament spot-light, or even a screened parabolic flood.

Colour photography of fabrics offers a number of interesting lighting possibilities. Especially with shiny light fabrics it can be effective to use coloured paper reflectors for the lightening of the shadow areas and thus add extra warmth or coldness to the original according to the colour of the paper reflector (*i.e.* blue = cold, red = warm, etc.). For normal straightforward rendering, however, all light sources must be of the same colour temperature and extreme contrast is to be avoided.

For special effects it is also feasible to add fine lines of lighting along the rims of a fold pattern of plain light fabrics by *contre-jour* spot-lighting which can be used with gelatine colour filters according to the desired colour effect.

Apparently, taking a certain amount of logical thinking for granted, texture rendering as such is not so difficult. But something more is needed. Most fabrics have a certain "touch" about them, and they must therefore not be set plainly on a table, but must rest loosely and in an unsymmetric but graceful fold pattern. This naturally confronts the photographer with new problems, because a low placing of his light will now produce big patches of shadow—shadow in which there is no drawing. The proper way to light a loosely draped fabric is to *place one's basic light source in such a way that it gives a rim light which accentuates rough outline pattern constructed by the fabric's natural folds.* This basic light must be retained as the strongest light and must dominate the whole lighting scheme. *The second light is a supplementary light which aims at picking up texture without over-powering the basic light.* Often it will be found that, here and there, shadows are still too dark, and that one must therefore employ *a third lamp (usually a diffused flood) which gives just enough relief to the shadow parts in question.*

Different types of fabrics obviously demand different kinds of treatment:

A ROUGH TWEED requires low angle lighting picking up the hairiness and rough-ness of the material. Tweeds therefore should be treated with hard low-angle lighting for the basic light.

SILK wants softness, glamour and sheen. We should therefore use a flood directly thrown on to it so as to create reflection which then should be supplemented by a vigorous spot-light effect (produced by a filament spot) in order to accentuate pattern and give "depth" to the image.

DAMASK should be treated in a purely reproductive manner because its main merit is the difference of tone created by a woven pattern. The same applies to any other fabrics (*e.g.,* chintzes, etc.) the sole pictorial merit of which is their pattern. It will be found that, in order to render a damask pattern successfully, the use of a contrast filter is desirable for black-and-white reproduction.

Leather

The material which demands the treatment most similar to that of fabrics is leather, especially the matt-surfaced varieties such as suede. The principal difference between lighting leather and lighting fabrics is that leather is usually photographed in the finished article, while fabrics are mostly photographed in bulk.

SUEDE LEATHER. The photographer has to distinguish between rough suede and smooth suede. Smooth suede is obviously a much more tricky subject. Its texture is so fine that it is difficult to "get hold of it" with lighting. Before one starts actually to build up one's lighting on a suede-leather object one must brush the surface so that all the "hairs" run in one direction—otherwise it will look patchy, an effect emphasised under strong light.

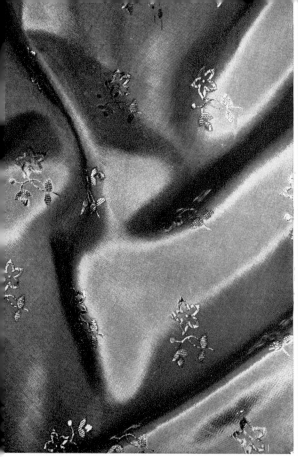

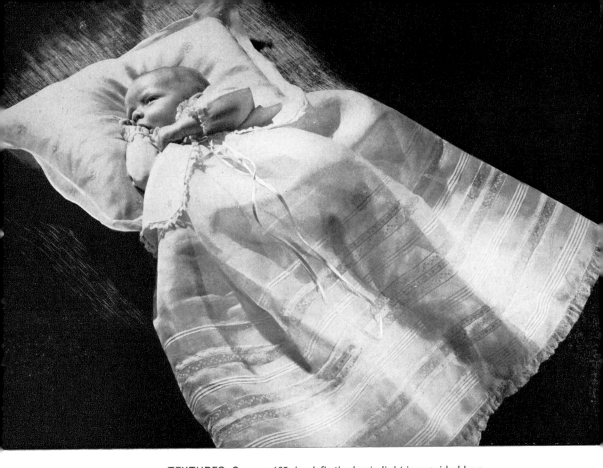

TEXTURES. *On page* 165, *top left:* the basic light is provided by a spot stressing fold pattern and sheen. Supplementary flood illuminates the large shadow areas, but it is carefully placed to retain sufficient depth in the folds. Phot: *W. Nurnberg (by courtesy of Harvey Nichols Ltd.). Top right:* furnishing fabric in bold light and shadow treatment. Basic lighting supplied by a spot giving pattern and rendering texture. Supplementary light, diffused frontal flood. Phot: *W. Nurnberg, London (by courtesy of The Studio Ltd.). Left:* flood lighting but a very appropriate one for rendering pattern. Phot: *H. Gorny, New York.*

A delightful baby study. The basic lighting is produced by a spot which gives to the picture its feeling of texture and warmth. Phot: *Doric Studio, London.*

Opposite: the lighting of this picture consists of two parts. Firstly, a normal 45° angle lighting against the camera, supplemented by a flood, and dealing exclusively with chair and cat. Secondly, a low angle spot to give a fireside effect and an added feeling of warmth, homeliness and comfort. The deep texture picked up by the supplementary light underlines this tendency. Phot: *W. Nurnberg, London (by courtesy of Lovell, Rupert & Curtis Ltd.).*

The opposite of rendering textures. A pure silhouette treatment giving intriguing pattern effect. Phot: *F. S. Lincoln, New York.*

LEATHER: *Left:* hogskin handbag. The "tooth and sheen" of the leather could be captured only by the combination of hard and soft lighting from various angles, which was achieved by the use of a carbon arc and an incandescent spot. Phot: *W. Nurnberg, London (by courtesy of Colman Prentice).*

Right: black suede handbag lit by carbon arc spot for basic lighting. An incandescent spot placed slightly underneath the table level gives depth to the bag without interfering with the background. Phot: *W. Nurnberg, London (by courtesy of Colman Prentice).*

169

PAPER. The treatment is a good example of spot lighting and what it can do. The predominance of the shadows gives a difficult material an almost sensorial quality. Phot: *W. G. Briggs, London*.

FLOWERS. Combination of direct rim lighting and purely reflected (indirect) "body" lighting. The limited use of the vigorous direct light on the edges of the flower and the unusual number of subtle tones in the centre give this flower picture considerable charm. Phot: *I. von Kuhnsberg, Danzig.*

Vigorous high lights give the flower its lightness. The hardness of the light is controlled so as not to lose texture and drawing. The shadows have been carefully diluted by the supplementary flood. Phot: *E. Landau, Paris.*

On page 172: the lighting is aimed more to give emphasis to a geometrical composition pattern than to render texture. Phot: *H. Gorny, New York.*

Suede, having a very "low texture" surface, demands a *lighting which meets it at an exceedingly oblique angle. For the basic light source carbon-arc lighting is the best.*

It is somewhat difficult to indicate the actual positions of the lamps, as these depend on the type of object, on the kind of suede-leather surface and on which way it has been brushed. It is therefore best to be open-minded and consider each individual problem as it comes. But when experimenting, *one must always view the object from the point at which the camera sees it, and from no other.* Especially when dealing with very fine textures and surfaces which produce a concentrated reflection, the smallest divergence of viewpoint makes all the difference.

With *black suede leather* one must realise that one has to create a grey-toned image because—obviously—a black surface can never show any texture at all. It will help, therefore, to surround it with a background which consists—at least to a certain extent—of deep black which will help to render tones of the suede leather to better advantage. The point is that black suede leather has a very low coefficient of reflection, while a white or light grey background would reflect a very considerable amount of light. We would require a considerable length of exposure time in order to get a satisfactory image of the suede surface; an exposure time which will naturally be far too long for the light background. By using a background of, let us say, a middle-grey tone, it becomes, under the influence of the long exposure, a lighter grey and at the same time the black suede surface will be correctly rendered.

HOGSKIN. Hogskin has certain photographic similarities to suede. Again the photographer has to distinguish between two kinds—rough matt and slightly glazed. (I am sure that leather experts will be deeply disgusted with this unorthodox classification. I hope they will excuse it, because I am looking at materials from a purely photographic point of view and am classifying them accordingly.)

The rough variety can be given carbon spot-lighting, meeting the surface at an oblique angle, and preferably shining towards the camera position. Diffused flood-lighting should be employed to control any excessive rendering of texture.

The glazed variety of hogskin demands a different treatment. The surface, being slightly glossy, not only reflects light, but also produces diffused reflections. The lighting should be so built that *the first lamp creates some kind of light-and-shadow pattern* which demonstrates the shape of the object—without actually rendering the texture of the object itself to any great extent. *The texture is now stressed by the supplementary light, a very diffused flood* usually being the most suitable. In certain circumstances a *second supplementary light will be necessary to "draw" in a few final highlight effects;* this should, however, be applied as sparingly as possible, so as not to make the leather surface look stony. The reader will have guessed by now that the second supplementary light thus described demands a *spot-light* of not too high an intensity.

CROCODILE. Again we are confronted with a fresh problem, and again must differentiate. Firstly, we have to deal with that kind of skin surface which is highly glossy, comparatively flat and intersected by a number of irregular lines. Especially when polished, it gives off very strong, and sometimes even concentrated, reflections. The second kind has a very horny and plastic surface moulding which catches light beautifully and produces substantial shadow forms.

We shall see in practice that crocodile always shows a certain amount of smooth surface which reflects. Our *basic light* should be a *spot,* and again aim at *determining light and shadow on the background and the shape of the object,* while the *supplementary light* has the task of *rendering the leather surface* in a typical manner. Again, a diffused flood is used for the supplementary lighting.

The amount of reflection to be produced on the surface depends not only on the grade of polish, but also on the requirements dictated by the photographer's client. Sometimes only very *soft reflections* are wanted, and in this case the supplementary light source will be a *paper-reflector* instead of a lamp.

LIZARD- AND SNAKE-SKINS. What interests us in lizard- and snake-skins is not so much texture as pattern and the obvious treatment indicated is one of "reproduction". Besides reproducing the shape of the object into which the skin has been manufactured, the photographer has to capture all the beautiful irregularities of the natural markings.

As we usually have to deal with three-dimensional objects, not the flat skin, adherence to the orthodox reproduction technique is not essential. We can therefore employ either spot- or flood-lighting from any angle which may seem appropriate as long as we take care that our lamps are so placed in relation to object and camera that we *do not obtain reflections which "fog" the leather surface* and thus eliminate the pattern impression.

SMOOTH CALF AND SIMILAR LEATHERS. In these smooth leathers—most commonly used for handbags, etc.—we have a perfect combination of "tooth and sheen"; it is here that the photographer has great scope to prove his skill in leather lighting. He can roughen or smooth the surface at will; *the more spot-lighting used the more toothy will the surface be,* while a soft and reflected lighting makes the surface smoother. The best solution is found, as usual, by combining both treatments without exaggerating either.

Before producing reflections on these kinds of leathers the shape and form of the object and the texture of the surface must first be properly rendered. The reflections should never be harsh and the best results are obtained by keeping them properly controlled.

Paper

Paper, with its great variety of texture and quality, and the fact that it is sometimes semi-transparent while on other occasions it presents itself as an opaque substance full of "body", presents a number of problems.

One must keep in mind that it is the job of the photographer to convey through an image the characteristics of the object. With semi-transparent papers the lighting has thus to render this characteristic, and should be such that no undue reflections are created to make the surface look "milky" or opaque.

In the case of opaque paper structures the photographer can light his subject in three ways: (1) In a manner which is appropriate to the familiar interpretation of paper in use; (2) To reproduce pattern by means of a flat reproduction technique; (3) To render texture by means of exceedingly oblique angle lighting and close-up treatment which create an image exaggerating the natural structure of the paper's surface.

Treatment 1 is usually applied to writing-paper, newspapers, magazines—in short, to all those papers where character is of only secondary importance, but where the range of its usefulness has primarily to be illustrated. Treatment 2 would be applied for printed wallpapers and decorative packing papers, etc., treatment 3 for heavy and rough paper surfaces such as embossed wallpapers and Lincrustas, the effectiveness of which relies on texture, or for corrugated papers, rough packing-papers and such like.

174

Opaque paper substances should be treated in much the same way as leather or fabric.

Flowers

Flowers are delicate things. Perhaps it is wrong to classify them as "inanimate" but, photographically they do present the same problems.

Here is one rule which should always be observed: the texture must never be exaggerated, but rendered in such a way that it does not differ from that impression perceived by the human eye in normal circumstances. Shadows should not be over-heavy, and the photographer should try to put in as many subtle half-tones as his subject is able to carry.

Soft lighting should therefore be used for the basic illumination. Hard lighting easily results in "chalky" effects and in a loss of modelling. When photographing flowers indoors we can either use artificial lighting only or artificial lighting mixed with daylight. But always it will be necessary to employ at least two light sources, one for the basic and the other (or others) for the supplementary effects.

The exact position of the light sources depends, of course, on the shape and type of the flower, and it will therefore vary accordingly. In principle, however, there are two main methods of basic lighting. Firstly, we have a *slightly elevated backlighting* giving rim light on the sides and on top of the object. These "against-the-light" shots render the shape of a flower beautifully and convey the whole delicacy of translucent blossom. It is necessary to supplement the basic light with a soft flood effect which brings drawing into the shadows and also avoids "heaviness". The second lighting method is a *side-lighting*, which, being supplemented by a flood, gives good form rendering especially when applied to non-translucent plants (cacti, etc.).

In both instances the basic light can be supplied either by a flood or a *diffused* spot or by the sun, the supplementary lighting by diffused daylight, diffused flood, white paper reflectors, silver paper reflectors or mirrors.

Artificial-light sources must *never be placed too near the flowers,* for they are easily affected by excessive heat. If absolutely essential, one can strengthen a flower by threading a piece of thin wire into its stem. At the same time a strong illumination is desirable, because some flowers turn towards the light very quickly, and only by short exposure-times can we avoid moved images.

Another important factor in flower photography is the treatment of backgrounds. A common mistake is to produce a background element which overpowers, through its realism, the delicate structure of the flower. What a chance the flower photographer has to infuse his picture with atmosphere, just by painting his background with soft

175

light and shadow effects! Altering the tone of the background is one of the means by which the character of the object or its significance can be emphasised.

REFLECTING SURFACES

The task confronting the photographer in the photography of textures is an obvious one: to create an image which illustrates the structure as well as the "character" of the texture. But when photographing reflecting and semi-reflecting surfaces his task is not so clear, because, although being reflecting to varying degrees, some of them must be treated in a way which conceals their reflectant faculty. This applies especially to polished wood.

On the other hand, we have reflecting surfaces the successful rendering of which depends solely on the rendering of just this faculty for reflection.

REFLECTIONS AND CATCHLIGHTS

The danger of a powerful reflection producing flare and halation is one against which one must always be on guard. Since a softening of the reflection will often destroy the texture and character of the material, it may be better to weaken the principal light source rather than diffuse it.

Where reflections have to be entirely suppressed—for instance, in photographing glazed pictures—or where a reproduction is required of, say, the patterning of a china ornament without any attempt at plasticity or modelling, a *Pola-screen is very valuable.*

This is a type of filter which depends upon a totally different principle from those so far considered. To understand the action of the Pola screen, we have to realise that normally, light vibrates in all directions. Light is, however, said to be *polarised* when it vibrates in one plane only. When ordinary light is specularly reflected from a smooth non-metallic surface it becomes polarised; consequently, by filtering out light which is polarised in that particular plane, and passing only unpolarised light, we can reduce the reflection or glare from a shiny object, permitting the texture to be seen by diffuse reflection.

Light reflected from a coloured subject is often in fact reflected from two surfaces—the actual pigment or dye and the surface of the material. The surface may reflect light of all wave-lengths and these, mingling with wave-lengths selectively reflected by the pigment give the appearance of a pastel or "desaturated" colour (desaturated = a hue diluted by white or grey).

Provided that the material is not metallic, these surface specular reflections will be more or less polarised, according to the angle of lighting incidence. By rotating a Pola-screen in front of the lens a position may be found in which a controllable proportion of this surface reflection is suppressed, resulting in a considerable increase in subject colour brilliance.

Polaroid consists of microscopic crystals, having the power of polarising light by transmission, which are embedded and correctly orientated in a transparent sub-

176

Mixed tungsten and electronic lighting. Background figures jumped during long exposure. Phot: *C. Hardacre* (*Polytechnic School*).

On page 177. Bounced and direct flash—one light from underneath plastic. Phot: *U. Finnila* (*Polytechnic School*).

On page 179. Single tungsten light source picture from side-light position. Phot: *R. Jones* (*London College of Printing*).

On page 180. Blast furnace. One head flash, with three PF100 blue bulbs plus available light. Phot: *A. S. Marshall* (*Stewarts & Lloyds Ltd.*).

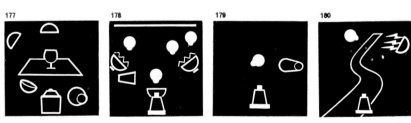

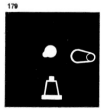

stance. A Pola screen consists of a layer of this material, cemented between glasses, and so mounted that it can be rotated to bring the plane of polarisation in the direction desired, which is best found by viewing the image on the focusing screen, or by holding the filter over the view-finder, and then mounting it on the lens at the same angle.

Polaroid has some neutral density, and necessitates an increase of exposure of three to four times.

But although in theory it is possible to rotate the Pola-screen to produce any desired suppression of reflections, this aim could quite often be more easily achieved by rearrangement of the lighting. For this reason, Pola-screens are more often used in outdoor photography, where the light source cannot be controlled to any extent, than in the studio.

Where any extensive area of specular reflection appears, some object will naturally be imaged as a catchlight. Not only should this object be appropriate to the subject—one would, for instance, not dream of imaging a factory window in the reflections of expensive silverware—but it must be regarded as part of the picture. Its lines must enhance, and not detract from, the modelling of the surface.

Wood

Wood (like leather) is usually photographed as an article of merchandise and not in the piece. The lighting of a wooden object has to achieve two ends. First, to reproduce as perfectly as possible the grain of the wood; secondly, to render the object itself in a plastic and attractive way. This twofold purpose must always be kept in mind, because a lighting which renders the grain successfully but fails to give the object "life" will for most practical purposes have failed. The same can be said of a lighting which succeeds merely in creating a plastic impression but neglects the pictorial interpretation of the wood's intrinsic characteristics. (It must be understood, however, that this applies to those objects where the rendering of the wood-texture is the main purpose of the picture.)

In photographing an object we always have to aim at producing an image which shows its three-dimensional form. We know that this can only be done by creating contrasting planes of light and shadow or, in other words, by rendering the receding parts of the object in a different tone-value from that of the front parts.

These requirements tell us the principles of lighting needed here. *The basic light should be such that it does not shine "flat" on the surface, but meets it at an angle.* The angle of light-incidence must be such in relation to the angle of camera-vision that reflections are not registered by the camera.

The supplementary lighting has the task of lighting to a desired degree the shadows produced by the basic light.

A further supplementary light can be employed to create well-placed highlight effects on the edges of the object—never, however, on the flat parts of the surface.

In order to reproduce wood-grain at its best it is necessary to employ *filters* in conjunction with panchromatic emulsions. Dark mahogany requires a light red filter, light mahogany and walnut a deep orange filter, while natural oak and similar woods are sufficiently rendered with a deep-yellow filter.

Pottery

Under this heading I include everything from china to earthenware.

Real china can be beautifully rendered by *against-the-light shots* which transmit to us the translucency of the material—*long shadows* in contrast with the delicate material enhancing its appeal.

With *unglazed earthenware* we must attempt to show as much of the texture as possible, and *use hard and contrasty lighting* to accentuate the feeling of "body", so characteristic of this "masculine" material. *Supplementary lighting should be used sparingly*—an exaggerated flattening of shadow parts would defeat our purpose. We can, however, give our object a *strong highlight*, best produced by a spot-light.

In glazed pottery we lose the texture and rely entirely on the rendering of the reflections. Here we have to be careful. Porcelain and china are materials of a certain delicacy producing soft reflections. It is therefore wrong for the photographer to create hard, concentrated reflections.

It follows that here we have to use *diffused light* sources or *bounced indirect* light for the creation of our reflection effects. In colour photography striking results can be obtained by using a softly coloured paper reflector, especially on glazed white china. This reflector should, however, be used from the side of the object, because a frontal reflector would tend to give an all-over colour cast upon the subject, instead of the desired small local highlight reflection.

Glassware

Let me say right away that even the most experienced photographer will have his surprises every time he starts photographing a glass object. The reason for this is primarily that we have not merely to deal with reflection and absorption, as in the other branches of still-life photography, but also to cope with refraction (see p. 29). We might even have to use the refractive faculty of glass for the creation of pictorial effects.

182

Photographically, glass calls for more imagination than any other material; it requires not only skill, but the ability to appreciate pictorial effects quickly; this all the more because no photographer can assess the shape, structure and effect of a refracted light pattern before he actually sees it.

There are three ways in which we can treat glassware. First by a straight-forward light and shadow treatment. Secondly by a treatment combining shadow and refraction pattern. Thirdly by means of shadow-free background photography.

The first treatment is used where we wish to show the glass in a naturalistic setting. The existence of a shadow which is linked up with the glass object helps to give the glass a certain substance and also gives, by its shape, information on the form of the glass object itself. As glassware is a material which naturally possesses a clear-cut and well-defined form, the shadow produced can also be well defined. A *carbon spot-light is therefore the ideal light-source* for this type of work. The shadow should be arranged so as to avoid any undue interference with the shape of the object.

It is obvious that the production of a definite shadow demands direct lighting and that, for this reason, there must always be a certain amount of refracted light which interferes somewhere with the pictorial composition. As these refractions cannot be eliminated, the light source must be placed in such a position that the refraction comes into a part of the picture where causing least disturbance.

The second treatment aims primarily at an interesting pictorial effect, and not at a truthful rendering. The most interesting effects of combined refraction and shadow pattern can often be produced by laying the glass object on a table instead of standing it upright. *Low-angle lighting often helps the effect.*

The third treatment is, in my opinion, the most appropriate for rendering plain glassware. It is beautiful in its simplicity, and the shadow-free method enables the photographer to infuse his background with a wide range of subtle tone-values which help to give atmosphere. I have already explained the technicalities of shadow-freep hotography in a previous chapter (see p. 109). It is obvious that here *the basic light will not be on the object, but on the background.* It can either take the form of varying tones produced by means of light deterioration, or by more definite pattern impression produced by spot-lighting.

One can help the rendering of shape by superimposing, on to the glass surface, reflections of different characters. For very deft and subtle reflections indirect lighting should be employed. For strong concentrated reflections the direct-lighting method is the appropriate one; here, however, one should again watch that the glass object is not used for "portraying" a lamp.

Photographically we have to distinguish between two kinds of silver: polished silver and matt silver. Basically, both demand the same treatment—namely, *indirect lighting.*

In *polished silver* a concentrated light source, providing direct lighting, has no effect whatsoever in respect of form-rendering or tone-rendering. The only result obtained when a lamp is placed in front of a silver object is that this lamp appears in the silver as an image, in the same way as it would appear in a mirror. We thus have to *use light sources which are extended enough to avoid being reproduced in the silver surface as definite shapes.* They must appear only as a light impression of varying tone. The only light source *suitable is a paper reflector*, and the brightness of the silver's surface depends on the tone-values imposed on to the paper reflector by means of light and shadow.

It must be realised that one cannot reflect an even tone, because this would give the material a lifeless appearance, which contradicts our familiar conception of the metal, and also render the object's form insufficiently.

Naturally it is much more difficult to create good lighting for round or curved silver objects. Sometimes it is necessary to construct a "tunnel" which is indirectly illuminated and encloses the object in a half-circle.

If the paper reflectors are large enough one can put them far away from the actual object. This results, of course, in a rapid fall of the light intensity, but it gives a greater chance to create a wide variety of tones on the reflector.

If very intense highlights are wanted—by means of a direct light— these *highlights must be kept very narrow and small,* and on no account must the image of the light source appear in the object.

The lighting for *matt silver surfaces* (or pewter, aluminium, etc.) is considerably easier. The rules applying to polished silver also apply, but one has not to be quite so careful in the use of one's direct light sources for the creation of additional highlight effects.

The best *highlight effects on matt silver are produced by diffused flood-lamps using a frosted filament bulb.*

It may be necessary to differentiate in the greys of our black-and-white picture between the colours of different metals. The obvious method is by the use of a contrast filter; thus a light blue filter—or equally the use of an orthochromatic emulsion—will cause copper or brass to reproduce notably darker than silver or steel.

But an exaggeration of this effect is undesirable; often a subtle difference in texture can be emphasised by the skilful arrangement of lighting.

184

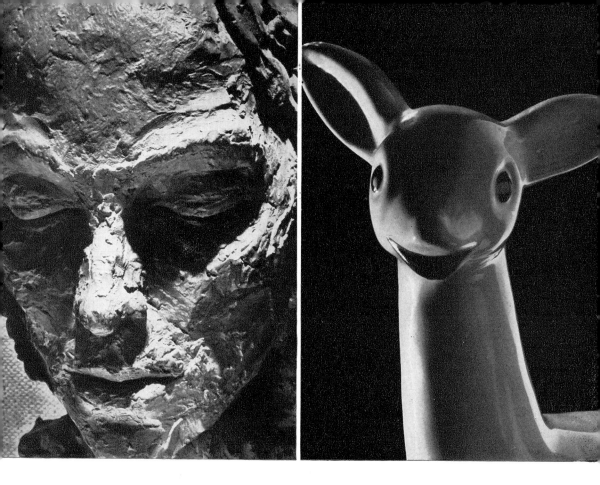

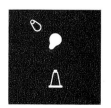

REFLECTING SURFACES IN ARTIFICIAL LIGHT. *Left:* This clay bust is lit in a very simple manner by a single spot light. The light coloured material by itself provides reflecting planes to dilute somewhat the shadows even where they are heaviest. Phot: *Ifor Thomas, London.*

Right: Double rim lighting is cleverly applied here to an inanimate subject. Phot: *Alexander, London.*

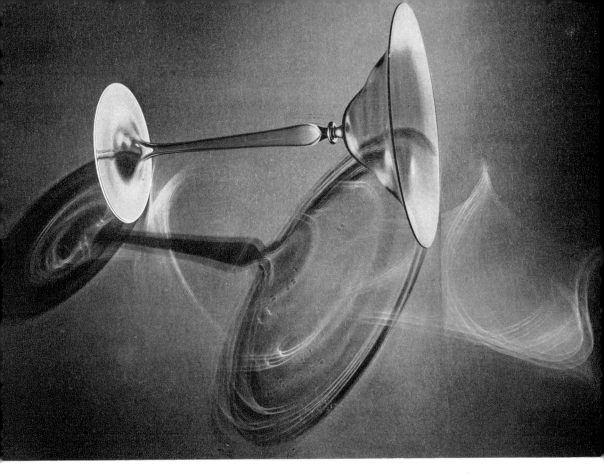

A good example of shadow and refraction treatment producing interesting patterns. It is easiest to produce this type of effect with the glass in a lying down position. Phot: *Peterhans, Chicago.*

On page 186: Basic light: spot on background; diffused direct lighting to produce reflections. Phot: *Alexander, London.*

On page 188, a single arc spot provides the shadows stressing a composition remarkable in its simplicity. Phot: *H. Althan, Stuttgart.*

On page 189: Effect as of daylight entering through windows, but in fact produced by spot lights reaching the subject through masks shaped accordingly. Phot: *H. Althan, Stuttgart.*

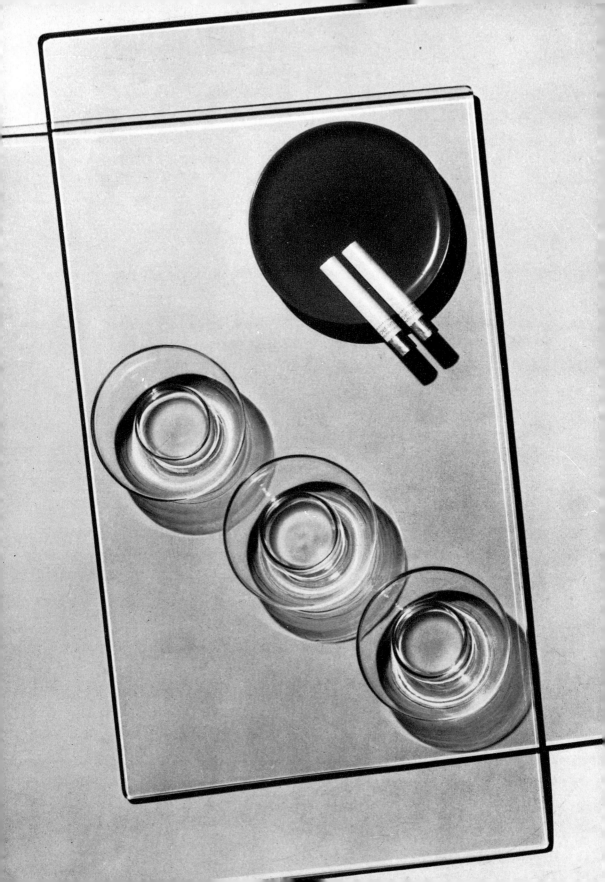

Basic lighting aimed at emphasising the composition and not at rendering the surface. The spot light is therefore placed in such a position that it does not give reflections. The surface quality of the silver is rendered by purely reflected (indirect) lighting. Phot: *W. Nurnberg, London (bv courtesy of Studio Ltd.).*

This is metal! The photographer has achieved an unusual brightness without getting glaring high-lights. Phot: *Lazi, Stuttgart*.

General illumination by a diffused flood and a few high lights put on by a spot light from high angle. Phot: *W. G. Briggs, London.*
Opposite: A symbolic still-life to epitomise plate work in heavy engineering. Main light 2-KW spot from the right; a low angle 500 watt spot light to pick out the chain's detail from the left. Phot: *Walter Nurnberg (by courtesy of Whessoe Ltd.).*

INDUSTRIAL PHOTOGRAPHY: Ordinary electric light and flash light combined. The light behind the subject helps to emphasise action. Phot: *H. Gorny, New York.*

Opposite: The hand had to be rim lighted to give utmost modelling to the rather flat form. At the same time wool texture had to be retained; the fill-in flood had, therefore, to be weak or strongly diffused. Phot: *W. Nurnberg, London (by courtesy of Hunt & Winterbotham).*

Opposite: Malt Kiln. A complicated scheme combining frontal lighting on background and figure with a strong direct "contre-jour" lighting from behind the figure to create atmosphere and depth. Modelling lighting is limited to the malt spread on the floor in the foreground. Phot: *W. Nurnberg, London (by courtesy of The Distillers Co.).*

NON-PHOTOGRAPHIC LIGHT SOURCES. The problem of the inclusion of a non-photographic light source in the picture is that mostly the actual photographic lighting has to make good the insufficiency of a more primitive light. This difficulty is cleverly overcome in our example by concentrating the beam of a spot on the globe of the oil lamp. (*Courtesy of Corning Glass Works, Corning, N.Y.*).

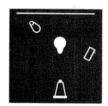

Opposite : Stacked glass tubes for fluorescent lamps. A straight-on view making use of both refractions and reflections to create the effect. Phot: *W. Nurnberg, London (by courtesy of Chance Bros. Ltd.).*

On page 197: Heavy gears. The nature of the subject with its many reflecting surfaces facing into so many different directions required a great number of individual light sources apart from the lamps required for the strong contour lighting on the figure. Phot: *W. Nurnberg, London (by courtesy of David Brown Gear Industries).*

199

Left: Supplementary lighting was necessary to equalise tone values and render detail. The halo round the candle was achieved by prolonged exposure without the flood on. Phot: *B. Malnasy, Budapest.*

Right: The candles here have a composition value only, as the lighting on the face obviously does not originate from them. Phot: *Judith Craig, London.*

LIGHTING IN ILLUSTRATIVE INDUSTRIAL PHOTOGRAPHY

Modern industry demands from the photographer not only a ready adaptability but a skill in lighting which is matched only by the versatility of the industrial scene itself.

Indeed, to be an industrial specialist (that is to be more than a commercial photographer who occasionally takes a few pictures in a factory) means to be a specialist of lighting every conceivable subject. He may be called upon to "manage" the vast expanse of a modern plate mill one day, a large group of assembly workers in action the next; then, close-ups of hands showing detail in manufacture, moving parts of machinery during production, or the gamut of textures which show the ever-changing aspect of a material in the making.

But this is not all. Sometimes his pictures may be expected to be cold but perfect reproductions for technical catalogues; or they have to reflect individual imagination and give a dramatic and significant interpretation of industrial enterprise for diverse outlets in press and prestige publicity.

Of latter years, more and more industrialists demand pictures which, when seen together, do not show a uniformity of technique but versatility of pictorial expression in keeping with the variety of subjects.

Now it must be understood that good industrial photography is not merely a matter of lighting. Indeed, it depends primarily on the ability of the mind to see a new vision in everyday subjects; it depends also on a flexible camera technique; it depends last but not least on an understanding, at least to some degree, of production and marketing methods of industry. But, when all this has been said, it is *lighting* of a particularly skilful and imaginative sort which will bring the pre-visualised ideas of the photographer and the hard facts of industrial production to life. Moreover, it is by means of lighting that important details are featured and irrelevant background elements suppressed. It is by means of lighting that we can make the seemingly insignificant look important, and a routine operation appear to be one of individual craftsmanship.

From all this it is quite obvious that the industrial photographer cannot rely on a small set of standard lighting schemes, for each new assignment will bring new problems to be solved. It is, therefore, of the utmost importance that the industrial photographer, in the progress of his career, has first mastered lighting of every conceivable type of subject; he must be a master of lighting for faces and figures, long-shots and close-ups, hands and still-life, including the whole gamut of textures and surfaces.

As I said above, industrial pictures may be used for very many different purposes, and it is, therefore, essential to ascertain not only the purpose which the pictures have to serve, but to find out which particular features of a machine are the most important. This information will determine our lighting methods.

Let us assume that we have to make a picture which has to show the greatest amount of detail merely to serve later on as a basis for technical retouching and annotation. We shall know that we have to curb any imaginative instinct in us and use lighting which does not hide any important detail by deep shadow. Sometimes we may find that one strong general flood from the front will be sufficient. At other times we may have to use two lamps or more in order to make such straightforward reproduction of machinery. The exact position of our lamps will depend much on the machinery itself. If it is of steel, we shall be forced into those lighting positions which avoid strong specular reflections. Thus the photographer, before placing his lamps, will do well to remember that the angle of light incidence is equal to the angle of reflection.

It is realised far too rarely that detail is destroyed just as much by excessive specular reflection as it is by shadow. It is certainly difficult to retain the surface texture of the various metals and at the same time to avoid halation due to the catch-lights of the polished surfaces. The use of a diffused light-source leads, however, to the loss of those finer features of texture which differentiate polished steel from plated brass or painted castings. If texture rendering of moving metal parts is of really overriding importance, it is a useful expedient to give a time exposure and to move the principal light source slowly during exposure in a direction which is parallel to the movement of the main catch-lights; for instance, when photographing a steel shaft the light-source should move in a direction perpendicular to the shaft or, in the case of a polished disc, the source may move circularly. The effect of such a movement can be studied easily before the exposure is made. In practice, however, such rendering of minute texture detail should be photographed on a stationary machine, when the ordinary techniques of lighting of metals are applicable.

As I have mentioned already, photography of machinery is sometimes considered to be merely a base for the efforts of a draughtsman and air-brush retoucher. Fortunately, photography is used for these purely reproductive purposes less and less as time goes on. Nowadays the industrialist looks to the photographer in ever increasing measure to provide him with pictures which give the beholder an impressionistic, imaginative yet accurate rendition. This new appreciation of the possibilities of creative photography is welcome, but

202

it demands from the photographer an even higher perfection of skill in lighting. No longer can the photographer rely on his faults being covered up by subsequent retouching, which can only destroy spontaneity and realism.

In the modern type of machine photography the photographer is allowed to find aesthetic satisfaction in the curve of a casting, in the patterns of gear wheels and coil springs; he may find beauty in the shape of stampings, in the sweep of handles, in the flight of perspectives, or in the complex cross patterns on a loom. But at the same time he must not just be "arty", but render essential details to the satisfaction of the industrial technician. Just because the imaginative photographer will leave much in shadow to attain a sense of drama, he must place his light particularly accurately on those parts which mean the most to the industrialists. In order to have lighting fully under control, the deployment of spot-lighting from many different angles must be fully mastered and, besides wide experience, the industrial photographer requires the equipment which enables him to change the angles of light incidence rapidly and efficiently. Sturdy double-telescopic stands, low-angle brackets, "barn doors" which can shield off some stray light and a compact distributor board for all the lamp-points are essentials for efficient working on location. The security regulations in industry rightly insist upon all electrical equipment being earthed.

The Figure in Industry

When discussing the principles of lighting relating to the dressed figure it was emphasised that angle lighting which gives good modelling to the figure was most important. This basic consideration becomes of great importance in industrial photography, where a figure is not photographed for its own sake, but as a part of a story. Flat lighting will destroy, but clear contour lighting emphasise, the *action* of a figure, and it is action, tension and realism which the human figure has to convey in an industrial photograph.

It is nearly always essential, therefore, to light a figure (or figures) separately from machine detail. This explains the necessity for a good number of spot-lights. The specification given on p. 60 gives a good idea as to what is required. You will note that large spotlights or massive flash equipment are recommended. These powerful items are essential, not only because they have a large light output and cover a wide field, but because they can be used from a good distance away and yet produce strong and effective lighting. This feature of lighting from a distance is important in industry because lamps placed too near would be included in any picture where we have to show some of the natural surroundings; moreover, only efficient lighting will enable us to arrest at least that movement which is caused by vibration of the floor.

The possible number of different industrial subjects is, obviously, infinite, and it would be futile indeed even to attempt to give detailed advice on how to plan lighting schemes. But one overriding principle for the lighting of figures in industry must be mentioned, namely, that as in the photography of groups, the placing of the highlights on the different elements of the picture must be such that it brings them together and does not separate them. Only in this way can the photographer convey that in industry men and machines are one; only thus can he emphasise that intensity of human effort and application of skill which are such important features in industrial publicity.

Hands in Industry

As we have seen before (p. 158) many different types of lighting may be suitable for the lighting of hands. In industrial photography the use of hands requires a very particular approach because hands are here never photographed for their own sake, but always to illustrate work in progress. In other words, not the hands as such but what they do is the feature of the picture. If we add that the tool is often smaller than the hands which use it, two things follow:

First, that lighting must be so used that the hands do not appear bulky and overpowering.

Secondly, that well-placed precision-lighting must be employed to emphasise the action of the hands.

Technically this means that flood-lighting and flat over-all illumination is rarely of any use. Indeed, it should be avoided whenever possible. Small spot-lights which enable us to apply rim lights to the contours of a hand are obviously the right light sources, and low-angle brackets will be an important part of the photographer's equipment.

Provided we take care to keep within the latitude of our negative material, hard and contrasty lighting is usually a good thing. It will help to convey that type of texture which we associate with a working hand, and which, by its realism, will make an industrial hand photograph all the more convincing.

The Long View

As we have seen, lighting in industry is never a simple matter but when we are called upon to create a dramatic black-and-white image of open general views, lighting can assume the complexity of a military operation. It must be realised not only by the photographer but also by his client that the more daylight that is in a factory the

204

more artificial lighting is essential. The reason for this is not to step up the level of illumination still further but to have sufficient precision lighting under one's control to accentuate certain areas or details and to give the picture the necessary sense of depth and three-dimensionality without which it will look dull and ordinary. As we have seen by the recommendations on p. 60 a great amount of equipment and electricity is involved and in practice I have seen even this doubled.

The photographer cannot possibly cope with these complexities by himself and the help of a competent electrician is always essential. Even then these "big" shots cannot be made at a moment's notice and careful preparations should be made in collaboration with all concerned ahead of the shooting.

Industry in Colour

The basic lighting techniques required for industrial colour photography do not differ in principle from those used in other photographic fields. But there are, of course, added difficulties, particularly the fact that it is impossible to mix daylight and incandescent lighting successfully. Thus one is often forced to use blue flash-bulbs—often in great numbers—to be able to work on daylight stock. But flash is not always the best method for subjects which require precision lighting shining acutely towards the camera lens (contre-jour effects). For long shots this difficulty may not apply and it is then mainly a matter of having a sufficiently high level of illumination which can of course be a very costly item.

Alternatively, it is frequently possible to exclude daylight sufficiently by means of tarpaulins and screens or to use the special Kodak Studio Filters Type E either in front of windows or light sources as already mentioned previously on p. 23 in the section "Colour Correcting Filters". Otherwise it will be necessary to work during hours of darkness.

There are, unfortunately, many who believe that because of the attractiveness of colour and also because of the necessity to control the contrast ratio it is not so important to light the subjects with imagination. It must be clear that this attitude can only produce a spate of very ordinary illustrations.

It is, of course, true that the monochrome medium demands often a far greater effort to replace the lack of colour with that particular drama and excitement which only light and shadow can give. But imagination is always essential whatever medium we may use.

General Considerations

Industrial photography taxes the ingenuity of the photographer yet further. The industrial photographer must pre-visualise his picture

P*

to a much higher degree than the photographer working in a studio or at home. It is impossible to hold up production in a factory merely in order that the photographer may shift his lamps around until he at last finds something which satisfies him. The industrial photographer must make up his mind quickly as to what he wants. He should, just as quickly, know how to go about putting his plans into action. Moreover, the industrial photographer may be quite a distance away from his various light-sources, sitting precariously perched on a girder, for instance, whilst his assistants below wait for clear and precise instructions how to move the lamps, not only to a given spot but also to a very definite elevation. The photographer who would insist upon climbing up and down to adjust his lamp positions would not only be an insufferable nuisance to his clients but prematurely an old man.

Therefore I urge those enthusiasts, who rightly look upon lighting in the live atmosphere of a factory as a most satisfying task, to be patient until they have mastered photographic lighting completely under the easier and more manageable conditions of a studio.

Only with practice and constant experience can knowledge become so well established that it is always "on tap" for spontaneous application.

Only after technique has ceased to be a worry and preoccupation can the mind visualise pictures fully. Only then we shall photograph more than the obvious—namely all those things which, although not yet visible to the eye, are already firmly fixed images within the creative mind.

Absorption, 26, 31
Actinism, 40
Action portraiture, 114, 147
Advertising photography, 59, 82, 147
Alternating current, 36, 37
Aluminium, 184
Amperes, 34, 35
Angström units, 12, 16
Architecture, 48
ASA ratings, 22

Background, 82, 106, 147, 159
Background projection, 82, 106, 110
Backlighting, 76, 175
"Barndoors", 58
Base of projection, 97
Basic light, 81, 121
Bi-post lamps, 55
Black, capacity for reflection, 29
Blotting-paper, 29
Bogus shadow, 89, 94, 99
Brightness, range of, 65, 67
Building up the lighting, 74

Calf-leather, 174
Camera technique, 28
Candle (as light source), 83, 84
Candle-power, 26
Capacitor, high voltage, 44
Capacity of installation, 35
Character studies, 115
Carbon-arc lamps, 40, 43, 44, 55
Cardboard (as reflector), 26, 57, 95
Catalogue illustration, 161, 202
Catchlights, 176
Central light, 76, 123
Chalk, as reflecting surface, 29
China, 182
Choke, 37
Colortran system, 56, 83
Colour, 20–25
Colour, aberrations, 55
Colour, balance, 22, 23, 41

Colour bands, 13, 14, 17
Colour cast, 20, 21
Colour compensating filters, 22
Colour contrast, 67, 147
Colour correcting filters, 23, 24, 205
Colour photography, 20–25
Colour printing filters, 24
Colour sensitivity (of negative materials), 16
Colour temperature, 20, 21, 23, 41, 43, 47, 48, 57
Colours, primary, 13
Complementary colours, 14, 17
Contrast filter, 17
Copper, 184
Correcting filter, 17
Crocodile leather, 164
Cross lighting, 76, 122, 124, 145, 147

Damask, 164
Dark-outline lighting, 121
Daylight, 21, 22, 71, 82, 83
Development (of negatives), 65, 66
Diffusers, 52, 56, 160
Diffusion, 52, 56, 108, 182
Dimmer, 37
Direct current, 36, 37
Distances, law of the square of, 26, 27, 30
Double-rim lighting, 144, 147
Dramatic photography, 75, 99, 121, 148

Earthenware, 182
Efficacy of illumination, 26
Electricity, cost of, 35, 59, 60
Electronic flash, 21, 40, 45, 72, 75, 114, 157
Electronic flash exposure meter, 45, 72
Emulsion of colour films, 20
Emulsion of monochrome negative, 13, 40, 66
Equipment (lighting), 59, 60, 203
Exposure, duration of, 22

Exposure, estimation of, 22, 65
Exposure-meters, 45, 68
Exposures, factors determining, 22, 65, 67, 70
Exposures, relative, 29, 40, 173

Fabrics, 163
Fashion photography, 60, 74, 75, 82, 147
Figures, lighting of, 76, 114, 145, 147, 203
Films (colour), 21
Film speeds, 53
Filter factors, 18, 69
Filters, 16, 19, 22, 28, 32, 40, 162
Flash bulbs, 21, 40, 45, 83, 108, 205
Flash, duration of, 45
Flash, electronic, 21, 40, 45, 72, 75, 114, 157
Flash factors, 70
Floodlighting, 49, 56, 99, 106, 108, 157
Flowers, lighting for, 175, 176
Foot-candle, 27
Foot-lambert, 27
Form-rendering, 75
Front lighting, 76
Front projection, 82
Fullface, 143
Fuses, 34, 35, 36

Giant screw lamps, 42
Glass, 29, 31, 111, 182
Glassplate (for shadow-free photography), 80, 111
Grey, reflecting capacity of, 29
Groups, lighting of, 147, 148
Guide numbers, 70

Half-silhouette, 81, 121, 124, 145
Half-watt lamps, 21, 40, 41, 55
Halogen lamps, 40, 43, 56
Halo-lighting, 84, 124
Hands, 158, 204
High-key, 76, 107
Hogskin, 164
Home lighting outfit, 58

Imitation cut-out, 109
Incidence, angle of, 27, 28, 97, 98
Industrial photography, 48, 54, 68, 74, 83, 147, 201, 203
Infra-red, 13, 16
Installation, electrical, 34
Integral reflector lamps, 42, 43, 56
International candle, 26
Inverse square law, 26, 27, 30

Joule, 44

Kelvin degrees, 20
Kilowatt, 35

Lamps, incandescent, 21, 40, 41, 43, 55, 56

Lamps, life of, 41, 42
Lampstands and fixtures, 61
Leather, 164
Light, absorption of, 28
Light balancing filters (colour), 23
Light, character of, 42, 48, 49, 54, 75
Light, colour of, 13, 14
Light, deterioration of, 42, 94
Light, direction of, 55, 75
Light, intensity of, 26, 27
Light, quality of, 40, 41, 55, 56
Light, quantity of, 26, 40
Light, reflected, 40, 57, 71, 108, 157, 182
Light, speed of, 12
Light, what it is, 12
Light filters, 16, 19, 22, 28, 32, 40, 162
Light sources (photographic), 16, 21, 39, 49, 83
Light sources (primitive), 40, 83, 84
Light-waves, 12
Lighting, bounced, 40, 51, 71, 108, 157, 182
Lighting, direct, 40
Lighting, indirect, 40, 57, 71, 108, 157, 182
Lighting, necessity of planning the, 76, 81, 206
Lighting schemes, 116
Lighting, three-dimensional, 107, 122, 150
Lighting, two-dimensional, 108
Lighting equipment, 49, 58
Lizard- and snake-skins, 174
Long-views, lighting, 204, 205
Low-angle bracket, 62, 160
Low-key, 57, 58, 76, 81
Lumen, 27

Machinery, photography of, 202
Millimicrons, 12, 13
Minus-blue, 14
Minus-green, 14
Minus-red, 14
Mirrors, 27, 57

Negative, colour as it affects the, 14, 16
Nudes, lighting for, 146

Off-centre lighting, 122
Ohms, 34
Ordinary emulsion, 16, 17
Orthochromatic emulsions, 16, 40
Orthopanchromatic emulsions, 16
Over-exposure, 65, 93, 109
Overhead lighting, 98
Overloading a circuit, 35, 36
Over-running a lamp, 36, 41

Paint, 29
Paintings, the production of, 161
Panchromatic emulsions, 16, 17, 19, 40
Paper, lighting for, 174, 175
Paper, lighting as reflecting surface, 29
Penumbra, 94
Pewter, 184

Photoflood bulbs, 42, 43
Photometric units, 26
Polaroid camera, 45
Pola-screen, 25, 176, 181
Porcelain, 182
Portraiture, 59, 76, 83, 107, 110, 114
Pottery, 182
Precision lighting, 52, 159, 204
Prism, 13
Profile, full, 81, 82, 121
Projection-base, 97
Projector lamps (bulbs), 52, 82

Quality of light, 40, 41, 55, 56
Quantity of light, 26, 40
Quartz iodine lamps, 40, 43, 56

Reciprocity failure, 22, 45
Reflection, action of, 21, 26, 31, 32
Reflection, angle of, 27, 29, 30
Reflection, coefficient of, (colours), 14
Reflection, coefficient of (surfaces), 26, 27, 29
Reflection, concentrated, 27, 38, 176
Reflection, diffused, 27, 38, 176
Reflection, specular, 27, 38, 176
Reflectors, flat, 27, 28, 57, 95, 163
Reflectors, spheric and parabolic, 48, 50, 123
Refraction of light, 29, 183
Rembrandt lighting, 124
Reproduction (black-and-white), 16
Reproduction (of colour), 13
Reproduction, lighting for, 161
Resistance (electrical), 36, 37
Rimlight, 75, 81, 121, 123, 141, 147, 164
Ring-light, 44, 48

Sealed beam lamp, 42, 43, 50
Semi-silhouette, 81, 121, 124, 145
Shadow, abstract capacity of, 98
Shadow, annexed, 95, 100, 105, 148
Shadow, cast, 93, 108
Shadow, concrete capacity of, 99
Shadow, definition of, 94, 96, 97, 99
Shadow, diluted, 94
Shadow, dominance of, 98
Shadow, form of a, 98
Shadow, hue of, 95
Shadow, isolated, 95, 105
Shadow, pure, 94
Shadow, shape and size of, 97
Shadow, tone of, 95, 96

Shadow-free background photograhpy, 107, 109, 183
Shadowless photography, 107, 147
Sidelight, 76, 121, 141, 142
Silhouette, 81, 99, 106, 124, 146
Silhouette-shadows, 105
Silk, 164
Silver, 184
Snakeskin, 174
Spectrum, 12, 41, 44
Spotlighting, 45, 49, 52, 58, 82, 99, 106, 115, 123, 157
Still-life, 59, 83, 105, 110, 111, 162
Studio, lighting equipment for, 36, 37, 59
Substances, colour of opaque, 31
Suede leather, 164, 173
Sunlight, 13, 14
Supplementary light and lighting, 81, 82, 121
Surfaces, reflecting, 27, 176
Surfaces, semi-reflecting, 27

Textures, 98, 115, 162
Theatrical photography, 115
Three-quarter face, 123
Top-lighting, 98
Transformer, 37, 57
Triangle light, 76, 122, 124, 145, 147
Tripack, 20
Tungsten filament lamps, 21, 40, 41, 55
Tungsten-halogen lamps, 40, 43, 56
Tweeds, 164

Ultra-violet, 13, 16
Umbra, 94
Umbrella reflector, 57
Under-exposure, 22
Under-lighting, 76, 142, 160
Under-running a lamp, 36, 41, 42
Units, electric, 34, 35
Unreality, 105

Velvet, 29, 162
Visualising, 76, 81, 206
Volts, 34, 35, 41, 42

Watts, 35
Wave-band, 13, 14, 17
Wave-length, 12, 13, 16, 17
Wedge spectogram, 16
White light, 13, 14, 17, 19, 20, 31
Wood, 181

MANUALS OF PHOTO TECHNIQUE

DEVELOPING

By C. I. Jacobson

"Developing" is the best established text and reference work on its subject in the world. Much of the book has been completely rewritten for the eighteenth edition. Particular attention is paid to colour development, quality control and the latest rapid access procedures. It also describes the theory of emulsion properties and of development, methods and apparatus, after-treatment and retouching. It covers everything from darkroom planning to after-treatment.

412 pp., 189 illus., 18th ed.

COLOUR FILMS

By C. Leslie Thomson

Deals with processing in detail, giving full, step-by-step instructions, together with formulae for the variety of solutions required. Films have certain minor variations that make processing different for each of them. There is useful information, too, on the after-treatment of films to improve colour rendering or remove unwanted casts, on the use of filters for special purposes, and on colour printing and the copying of slides.

280 pp., 66 illus., 6th ed.

EXPOSURE

By W. F. Berg, DSc., F.Inst.P., F.R.P.S.

This standard work has been entirely revised and brought up to date for the 4th edition. A major addition is a chapter on Latent-Image Formation. It helps the reader to pick the right tools and materials, to suit filters to film and subject, to determine the correct exposure and to decide what is best for each occasion. It tells you "how" and does it so that you will readily understand "why".

458 pp., 102 photographs, 110 diag., 4th ed.

PHOTOGRAPHIC OPTICS

By Arthur Cox

Thoroughly revised and updated, this latest edition has been enlarged to include a new section about micrographics. The principal purpose of the book is still to enable practical photographers to discriminate between lenses as intelligently as they choose films and filters. It fully explains the basics as well as the increasing sophistication of the subject. No lens is perfect, but it shows that modern lenses can behave perfectly if correctly used.

490 pp., 171 illus., 15th ed.

ENLARGING

By C. I. Jacobson and L. A. Mannheim

The present revised edition is a complete and thorough reappraisal, bringing the material fully up to date. It covers black-and-white as well as colour enlarging, and ranges from negative quality and principles of enlarging and darkroom equipment to advanced systems of exposure measurement, colour control and special processes and processing. A practical guide for the seriously interested amateur and also a comprehensive handbook for the professional.

528 pp., 390 illus., 21st ed.

COLOUR PRINTS

By Jack H. Coote

An extensively revised and thoroughly up-to-date edition of the most authoritative work on its subject. You will find advice on colour enlargers, darkroom layout, voltage control, filters, exposure estimation, processing, finishing, fault finding and every aspect of making successful colour prints. Simple step-by-step instructions, formulae and diagrams help you to follow the intricacies of a complicated but not too difficult task.

274 pp., 101 illus., 6th ed.

RETOUCHING

By O. R. Croy

Expert retouching can heighten or reduce contrast, remove blemishes, balance tones, sharpen or soften outlines, clear fuzzy backgrounds and improve or even radically alter colour rendering. Professor Croy tells you what tools and materials to use and how to use them. In this revised edition, there is a completely new chapter on retouching colour prints and transparencies.

192 pp., 304 illus., 4th ed.

BASIC SENSITOMETRY

By L. Lobel and M. Dubois

Today sensitometry overlaps into fields of printing, processing, colour sensitivity, filters, graphic arts, sound films and X-rays. Material on the modern advances has been considerably expanded in this revised edition. Nevertheless, the basically simple approach has been maintained. From this extremely clear-cut text the student will easily be able to translate the various graphs and curves on data sheets of films and papers into useful information.

272 pp., 171 illus., 2nd ed.

BOOKS ON CAMERA TECHNIQUE

VIEW CAMERA TECHNIQUE
By Leslie Stroebel

This is the first thoroughly comprehensive modern work to be devoted to all types of studio and field cameras – from the newest to the oldest. It analyses every feature and details every use. The most modern applications of the view camera in industrial, commercial, architectural and fashion photography are covered in separate illustrated sections. The author is Professor of Photography at the Rochester Institute of Technology New York.

312 pp., 659 illus., 2nd ed.

PORTRAIT PHOTOGRAPHY: HOW AND WHY
By Mary Allen

A complete study of portrait photography which shows the photographer how to express his ideas from a sound basis of knowledge and experience. It explains the fundamental reasons for the rules governing lighting, composition and subject matter, so he may become free of them. Mannerisms, psychology, modern enlarging techniques and interpretation of the character in terms of colour are fully discussed.

292 pp., 269 photographs, 24 diag.

CREATIVE PHOTOGRAPHY
By O. R. Croy

Photography is not merely a means of copying life on the surface. It can get right down to essentials. It can enable the photographer to conjure up forms and shapes of limitless variety and to present his own individual ideas of what life is all about. It is this creative ability with which Professor Croy is concerned in this book. Read his instructive text and study his methods.

160 pp., 127 illus.

CAMERA COPYING AND REPRODUCTION
By O. R. Croy

Shows the photographer how to use his normal camera to produce records and duplicates, and covers all the relevant techniques, including simple contact copying, camera copying, the use of films, filters and lighting, as well as exposure, processing and working by ultra-violet and infra-red radiation. Individual sections deal with the approach to different kinds of originals and methods and techniques of systematic documentation.

256 pp., 101 illus.

LIGHT ON PEOPLE
By Paul Petzold

Here is a book on photographic lighting – with a difference. In the past indoor lighting had to be contrived and outdoor light just accepted. Films, lenses and cameras of today have vaulted across the division. Light is no longer a limitation and certainly not a straitjacket. It is a creative tool irrespective of whether you use it indoors or outdoors, for black and white or colour. This book reflects the new freedom of spirit.

152 pp., 178 illus.

THE PHOTOGUIDE TO PORTRAITS
By Günter Spitzing

This is a straightforward guide to taking good and attractive portraits in all kinds of light. It is written for the amateur photographer in clear and lively language. The inclusion of pertinent references to topical portrait photography gives it appeal for the general reader. It will enable him to understand the tricks of the trade, and to divine the real person behind the façade which he sees on TV at the cinema or in the newspapers.

Casebound and paperback, 180 pp., 145 illus.

DESIGN BY PHOTOGRAPHY
By O. R. Croy

Professor Croy has for many years experimented to explore multitudes of approaches to the frontiers where photography and graphic design overlap to yield a new world of imagery. In this book he covers a wealth of unorthodox techniques which can be used to reinterpret the elements ordinary negatives are made of, to produce selective and often startling effects that artists might dream of.

184 pp., 432 illus.

CAMERA CLOSE UP
By O. R. Croy

In this book Professor Croy explains the technical and practical problems involved in dealing with animals and plants, insects and blossoms, coins, medals, and a multitude of other live and lifeless objects, at close and closest range. It covers the various aspects of near focusing, depth of field, close-up exposure and the peculiarities of lighting, arranging and locating subjects under the magnifying glass.

228 pp., 196 illus.

THE FOCAL
ENCYCLOPEDIA
OF
PHOTOGRAPHY

2,400 articles: $1\frac{3}{4}$ million words
1,936 pages, 450 photographs, 1,750 diagrams

Revised edition in two-volume set.
Desk edition also available.

THE FOCAL ENCYCLOPEDIA will do the job of a whole library. These two volumes hold the right answers to any question on photography—ready for prompt reference. They contain more information than many books put together. Much of it could not easily be found elsewhere. A great deal of it has never been published before.

THE FOCAL ENCYCLOPEDIA covers completely the vast technology of photography and follows up all its uses for picture making. It defines terms, identifies personalities and quotes rules. It recalls past developments and records the present state of progress all over the world. It sums up scientific theory and instructs in up-to-date practice. It presents all the facts that matter, explains "why" and shows "how". It hands out advice based on first hand knowledge, expert skill and reliable authority.

THE FOCAL ENCYCLOPEDIA is specially written in plain, readable and commonsense English. It was carefully planned and set out in alphabetical order for easy reference. You will be able to find, instantly master and put to good use, all the information you need from whatever angle you look for it.

THE FOCAL ENCYCLOPEDIA is the only work of its kind in the world. A unique, up-to-date and universal source of photographic knowledge and an unfailing tool of practical help to any photographer, student of photography, professional and amateur, advanced and beginner alike.

THE FOCAL ENCYCLOPEDIA can take the place of a photographic library; and no library is complete without it.

See it at your bookseller's or photographic dealer's or write for full prospectus to Focal Press